THE FACE OF THE RECONCILER:

SHARING THE LA SALETTE
CHARISM OF RECONCILIATION

BY FR. NORMAND THEROUX, M.S.

LA SALETTE COMMUNICATIONS CENTER PUBLICATIONS
947 PARK STREET
ATTLEBORO, MASSACHUSETTS 02703
WEB SITE: WWW.LASALETTE.ORG

D1127065

TABLE OF CONTENTS

Prologue

The Story of the La Salette Apparition

On Saturday, September 19, 1946, a "Beautiful Lady" appeared to two children, both from Corps, in France Alps: Maximin Giraud, eleven year old, and Mélanie Calvat, almost fifteen, who were watching their herds on the slope of Mont Planeau (alt. approx 6,000 ft.), not far from the village of La Salette. In a little hollow, the suddenly noticed a globe of fire – "as though the sun had fallen on the spot." Within the dazzling light they gradually perceived a woman, seated, her elbows resting on her knees and her face buried in her hands.

The Beautiful Lady rose, and said to the children in French:

Come closer, my children; don't be afraid. I am here to tell you great news.

She took a few steps towards them. Maximin and Mélanie, reassured, ran down to her and stood very close to her.

The Beautiful Lady wept all the time she spoke. She was tall, and everything about her radiated light. She wore the typical garb of the women of the area: a long dress, and apron around her waist, a shawl crossed over her breast and tied behind her back, and a close-fitting bonnet. Along the hem of her shawl she wore a broad, flat chain, and from a smaller chain around her neck there hung a large crucifix. Under the arms of the cross there were, to the left of the figure of Christ, a hammer, and, to the right, pincers. The radiance of the entire apparition seemed to emanate from this crucifix, and shone like a brilliant crown upon the Beautiful Lady's head. She wore garlands of roses on her head, around the edge of her shawl, and around her feet.

The Beautiful Lady spoke to the two shepherds. first in French, in these words:

If my people refuse to submit, I will be forced to let go the arm of my Son. It is so strong and so heavy, I can no longer hold it back.

How long a time I have suffered for you! If I want my Son not to abandon you, I am obliged to plead with him constantly. And as for you, you pay no heed!

However much you pray, however much you do, you will never be able to recompense the pains I have taken for you.

I gave you six days to work; I kept the seventh for myself, and no one will give it to me. This is what makes the arm of my Son so heavy. And then, those who drive the carts cannot swear without throwing in my Son's name. These are the two things that make the arm of my Son so heavy.

If the harvest is ruined, it is only on account of yourselves. I warned you last year with the potatoes. You paid no heed. Instead, when you found the potatoes spoiled, you swore, and threw in my Son's name. They are going to continue to spoil, and by Christmas this year there will be none left.

Mélanie was intrigued by the expression, *pommes de terre.* In the local dialect, potatoes were called *las truffas.* She looked inquiringly at Maximin, but the Beautiful Lady anticipated her question.

Don't you understand, my children? Let me find another way to say it.

Using the local dialect, she repeated what she had said about the harvest, and then went on:

If you have wheat, you must not sow it. Anything you sow the vermin will eat, and whatever does grow will fall into dust when you thresh it.

A great famine is coming. Before the famine comes, children under seven will be seized with trembling and die in the arms of the persons who hold them. The rest will do penance through the famine. The walnuts will become worm-eaten; the grapes will rot.

At this point the Beautiful Lady confided a secret to Maximin, and then to Mélanie. then she went on:

If they are converted, rocks and stones will turn into heaps of wheat, and potatoes will be self-sown in the fields.

Do you say your prayers well, my children?

— III —

"Hardly ever, Madam," the two shepherds answered candidly.

Ah, my children, you should say them well, at night and in the morning, even if you say only an Our Father and a Hail Mary when you can't do better. When you can do better, say more.

In the summer, only a few elderly women go to Mass. The rest work on Sundays all summer long. In the winter, when they don't know what to do, they go to Mass just to make fun of religion. In Lent they go to the butcher shops like dogs.

Have you never seen wheat gone bad, my children?

They answered, "No, Madam."

The Beautiful Lady then spoke to Maximin.

But you, my child, surely you must have seen some once, at Coin, with your father. The owner of the field told your father to go and see his spoiled wheat. And then you went, and you took two or three ears of wheat in your hands, you rubbed them together, and it all crumbled into dust. While you were on your way back and you were no more than a half hour away from Corps, your father gave you a piece of bread and said to you: "Here, my child, eat some bread while we still have it this year; because I don't know who will eat any next year if the wheat keeps up like that."

"Oh, you," answered Maximin, "Now I remember. Just then, I didn't remember it."

The Beautiful Lady then concluded, not in dialect but in French:

Well, my children you will make this known to all my people.

Then she moved forward, stepped over the stream, and without turning back she gave the injunction.

— IV —

Very well, my children make this known to all my people.

The vision climbed the steep path which wound its way towards the Collet (little neck). Then she rose into the air as the children caught up to her. She looked up at the sky, then down to the earth. Facing southeast, "she melted into light." The light itself then disappeared.

On September 19, 1851, after "a precise and rigorous investigation" of the event, the witnes¬ses, the content of the message, and its repercussions, Philibert de Bruillard, Bishop of Grenoble, pronounced his judgment in a pastoral letter of instruction. He declared that "the apparition of the Blessed Virgin to two shepherds, September 19, 1846, on a mountain in the Alps, located in the parish of La Salette,... bears within itself all the characteristics of truth and that the faithful have grounds for believing it to be indubitable and certain."

In another pastoral letter, dated May 1, 1852, the Bishop of Grenoble announced the construction of a Shrine on the mountain of the apparition, and went on to add:

> "However important the erection of a Shrine may be there is something still more important, namely the ministers of religion destined to look after it, to

receive the pious pilgrims, to preach the word of God to them, to exercise towards them the ministry of reconciliation, to administer the Holy Sacrament of the altar, and to be, to all, the faithful dispensers of the mysteries of God and the spiritual treasures of the Church.

"These priests shall be called the Missionaries of Our Lady of La Salette; their institution and existence shall be, like the Shrine itself, and eternal monument, a perpetual remembrance, of Mary's merciful apparition."

The first priests imbued with the spirit of the Apparition and who devoted themselves to the service of the pilgrims, felt from the beginning the call to and the need for religious life. Six of them pronounced their first vows on February 2, 1858, in accordance with their provisional Constitutions, adapted in 1862 to include Brothers. From that time, Fathers and Brothers have constituted one religious family.

MARY'S APPARITION AT LA SALETTE is a modern-day reminder of an ancient truth: that Mary constantly intercedes for us before God; that she is the Reconciler of Sinners, calling us back to the message and way of her Son, Jesus.

THE LA SALETTE MISSIONARIES are founded upon the reconciling message and mission of this Apparition of Mary. Their congregation numbers about 1,000 priests and brothers as well as several hundred La Salette Sisters. They are motivated by their charism and ministry of reconciliation and make Mary's message known to all her people in over thirty countries around the world.

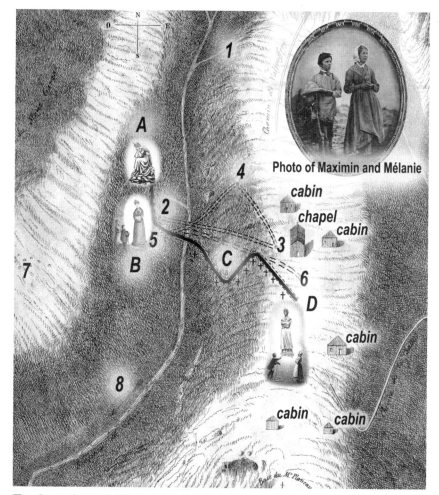

Photo of Maximin and Mélanie

Explanation of Site of the La Salette Apparition, Sept. 19, 1846:

Mary: A: the miraculous fountain where Our Lady was seated, weeping; B: place of their conversation; C: path marked by crosses where Our Lady walked (130 feet); D: the place where Our Lady disappeared.

Children:1: the Men's Spring where the children ate; 2: area where they fell asleep; 3: the place where the children looked for their cows; 4: place from where the children saw the globe of light; 5: place of conversation and path the children took to top of knoll (5-6); 6: where children saw Our Lady disappear; 7: the area where the cows were grazing; 8: animals' fountain.

chapel: the provisional chapel; **cabin**: the five cabins built after the Apparition;
Note: solid line indicates Our Lady's path; dotted lines indicate the childrens' path.

Introduction:
For the Love of a Gem

"The famous New York diamond dealer, Harry Winston, heard about a wealthy Dutch merchant who was looking for a certain kind of diamond to add to his collection. Winston called the merchant, told him that he thought he had the perfect stone, and invited the collector to come to New York and examine it.

"The collector flew to New York and Winston assigned him a salesman to meet him and show him the diamond. When the salesman presented the diamond to the merchant, he described the expensive stone by pointing out all of its fine technical features. The merchant listened and praised the stone but turned away and said: 'It's a wonderful stone but not exactly what I want.'

"Winston, who had been watching the presentation

from a distance, stopped the merchant going out the door and asked, 'Do you mind if I show you that diamond once more?' The merchant agreed and Winston presented the stone. But instead of talking about the technical features of the stone, Winston spoke spontaneously about his own genuine admiration and what a rare thing of beauty it was. Abruptly, the customer changed his mind and bought the diamond.

"While he was waiting for the diamond to be packaged and brought to him, the merchant turned to Winston and asked, 'Why did I buy it from you when I had no difficulty saying no to your salesman?'

"Winston replied, 'That salesman is one of the best men in the business and he knows more about diamonds than I do. I pay him a good salary for what he knows. But I would gladly pay him twice as much if I could put into him something that I have and he lacks. You see, he knows diamonds, but I love them'" (1).

That story illustrates one of the single greatest principles of persuasion: People are far more persuaded by the depths of your beliefs and emotions than any amount of logic or knowledge you possess.

The preceding anecdote could be a modern parable. Harry Winston had a gift. One could say that diamonds were his 'charism.' He could have been taken up with rare coins, stamps or shells but his passion was the beauty and splendor of diamonds. That love was a gift. Gems transformed his whole life. He converted that love into a livelihood because he was able to communicate some of his 'obsession' on to others. He was able to sell diamonds because he loved them.

RECONCILIATION IS A GEM OF A CHARISM. Only people who love it, who communicate their love of it, can pass reconcilliation onto others. A charism is pure grace, pure gift. It is a love endowment and the result of a choice by God and bestowed on a person or group of persons to fulfill a special mission within the Church. It is a call and a sending. It is not a specific work or ministry, but a spirit, a conviction, an inspiration, an attitude by which a given life and calling are lived out, by which a given ministry or service is accomplished.

When we say, for example, that reconciliation is the charism of the Missionaries of La Salette, we do not mean that all La Salette persons are committed to a very defined and limited ministry. We mean that whatever ministry they are engaged in, whatever life they have embraced, they live and serve in a spirit of reconciliation.

The charism of a congregation, then, is a founding grace given to a person or a group of persons. Often, that grace is given to one person, the founder, and he or she gathers people together who, in their prayer, daily work and ministry to the Church, will be guided by that special founding grace. Sometimes this charism is given to many people who become the expressions of that grace in the life of a foundation.

The charism of a Community may also come to a founder (or founders) through a founding experience. We may assume that for the La Salette Missionaries, the apparition of Our Lady at La Salette was a founding experience. Mary did not found the Congregation but her apparition became the occasion of its founding.

RECONCILIATION AS A CHARISM

THE TITLE GIVEN TO OUR LADY OF LA SALETTE – RECONCILER OF SINNERS – describes the reason for her apparition on the Holy

Mountain. The first written testimony applying the title of "Reconciler of Sinners" to Our Lady of La Salette dates back to September 6, 1848 in a document called the Perrin Manuscript. Father Louis Perrin was pastor of the parish of the village of La Salette from 1846 to 1852. This title was used in relation to the Confraternity of Our Lady of Seven Dolors founded within the parish in May, 1848, by Father Perrin and his priest-brother Jacques-Michel who served as his temporary assistant. This is the origin of the title as we know it, but the substance of it – conversion, return to the will of God – is therein aptly described.

Fr. Louis Perrin, Pastor of Parish of La Salette from 1846 to 1852

Clearly, the ministry of reconciliation is the work of the universal Church and of every baptized person. Indeed, every ministry in the Church belongs to the entire Church. The Missionaries of Our Lady of La Salette have received the charism of reconciliation from the very words of Our Lady's message at La Salette. The Lady first spoke the message but its root origin was the Son himself. The grace of La Salette is the grace of reconciliation, the standing invitation to return to the Father. The ministry exercised by the Missionaries and those who are associated with them is a service performed for the entire people of God. Through the witness of their lives and their various works, the Missionaries labor for the return of every member of the people of God to conversion and peace.

FOLLOWING MARY AT LA SALETTE

RECONCILIATION IS AN IDEA AS WELL AS AN IDEAL. Concretely it is most often applied to individuals in specific situations. Whoever would perform this ministry needs to examine the manner, style and spirit with which Christ himself exercised it in the gospels and how Mary performed it at La Salette on that Saturday afternoon in 1846. A study of Christ's own ministry of reconciliation in the gospels would be too great an undertaking. It is indeed, a complete journey through the New Testament.

In a more limited way, I will read through the beautiful Lady's discourse at La Salette and try to derive from her words some guidelines for living out the mystery and exercising the ministry of reconciliation. Since the charism is the moving force behind the ministry we can hope to see how the Mother of God exercises that charism and thus find a model to emulate and footsteps to follow. She lives the charism we constantly strive to bring into our lives.

I will attempt a comment on the salient passages of the La Salette discourse and I remain fully aware that such work is never done, nor is it ever good enough to put before the flint-eyed scrutiny of knowledgeable confreres.

I thank God for giving us the likes of Chesterton, who said: "What is worth being done is worth being done badly."

1

Come Closer, My Children

THE LA SALETTE RECONCILER REMAINS CLOSE TO THE PEOPLE and reaches out to all of them. He seeks out those who never appear at any function, who are far away, the alienated. He lets them know that they are desired, invited, wanted, not because they are prayerful, cultivated people, but because they are valuable in themselves.

The Lady gave a vivid example of this kind of seeking. Maximin and Melanie were the "ideal" unchurched people. As far as the Church and the world were concerned they lived in the black hole of oblivion. They were the alienated, people who were totally indifferent to the existence of God and Church. They were textbook examples of uninterested and uninteresting people – normally undesirable – practically useless in any church organization. They were invited not just to come around but also to come near. They were summoned to intimacy. The Lady chose Maximin and Melanie in order to tell the world that God loves and chooses people not by virtue of rank or accomplishment but in view of a special mission God has reserved for them. They were asked to belong. *People love to be asked.* They love to belong to something or someone greater than themselves. The Lady's first words corresponded to a very normal human desire – more than that – a craving to belong and to be used importantly and especially lovingly.

Throughout the many centuries of turbulent relationship between God and people, God has always invited people to return. No offense was able to create the definitive break. No matter how many bridges humanity blew up, God always rebuilt them. The Lord is always and in many ways saying, "Come near."

THE THREAD

There is an old Rabbi's teaching that states that our relationship with God is like a thread joining God and us together. Each time we sin the thread is broken and God alone can tie the two ends together again. But then, the thread is shortened.

Reconciliation, besides renewing the bonds between two parties, very frequently deepens them and strengthens intimacy.

2

DON'T BE AFRAID

A few years ago a survey revealed which emotion people experienced most often. A large number mentioned fear and anxiety. There is a lot of fear in the world and much of that fear is fear of God. Fear comes from the unknown and God is the Great Unknown. God is mysterious. People think of God as all-powerful and judge: an awesome combination. There is a just fear of God which is not abject cowering. The fear of God spoken of in the Scriptures is, for the most part respect, honor, reverence, deference.

People cannot "come closer", cannot be reconciled in fear. Fear must go and it won't go easily. Many were born and raised in a straightjacket of fear about religion: a punishing God – "God will get you for this, you wait and see!" – events, natural phenomena, diseases, accidents became deeds right from the avenging hand of God. There is nothing quite like fear to alienate and persuade someone to keep a safe (!) distance from all that is "God."

The reconciler's first task is to break fear. Manner, style, respectful familiarity with God and the things of God, reassurance about the certainty of reconciliation from a loving Father can do wonders to dispel apprehension.

La Salette is not a new revelation. Revelation ended with St. John the Evangelist. This in no way prevents an apparition like La Salette to reveal thoughts of God. The God shown to us here is One who is concerned about people's fruit and harvests and dislikes famine. This is a God who weeps and gets angry when people blow their chances for happiness.

We can only imagine what Maximin and Melanie felt when they saw that fiery globe of light in the ravine.

> "They could hardly believe their eyes, so bright was she: her body, her hands so drenched in light. 'O moun Diou!' screamed Melanie in her native dialect. The warnings of grandmother Caron rushed to her mind in a flash: 'Little one, you laugh at those who pray, do you? Well, some day you'll see something!' Frightened, she let her stick fall to the ground. No less frightened, Maximin still found the courage to reassure her. 'Keep your stick, Melanie, I'm keeping mine. If it harms you, I'll give it a good whack!' Still dazed, Melanie picked up her stick.

> "Together, they stared transfixed as the Lady stood erect in the oval light, her face visible now, her hands in her long sleeves crossed in front of her. Immediately, they heard a voice as of a mother calling 'Come near, my children. Do not be afraid I am here to tell you great news.'

> "Their fear vanished then and there. That voice penetrated them like music. They ran to the bottom of

the ravine, crossing the brook. With sovereign grace the Lady made a few steps toward them. The boy at her left, the girl at her right, they were so close that they almost touched. A person could not have passed between them and the Lady" (2).

As they told the Story of the Apparition the children were quick to boast that they had come so close to the Lady that no one could have passed between them and her. The Lady told them to come close.

Ministers of the Gospel also tell people to come close. They hope for it not only in the solitude of room or chapel, but let it be known that the Church does want them closer. The Lady wanted Maximin and Melanie as they were and where they were.

She came to meet them in the very fabric of their lives. She came to the mountain to find them. She spoke to them in their language. She did not speak to them in abstract puffs of rhetoric. She spoke of rotting walnuts and potatoes and grapes, of spoiling wheat and cursing cart drivers, of a boy and his father strolling on a friend's farmland watching wheat turn to dust in their hands.

Some say that La Salette is as outdated as the "plug and plow." But didn't Jesus speak of fig trees and mustard seeds and houses built on sand, of lost sheep and lost sons and signs in the seasons announcing times for sowing and harvesting? The Lord is always close to people.

The very first purpose of the Lady's words is to put the children at ease in the presence of the stunning scene before their eyes. They were small, young, vulnerable and helpless. And they were alone. The Virgin's first concern was to dispel their fear and induce a mood conducive to absorbing calmly what they were about to see and hear.

But we may easily see in these words an allusion to people's fear of the divine. From time immemorial, people have been trying to appease the gods as well as God. They have been attempting to placate a highly whimsical, moody and often cruel Fate. These people are firmly convinced that everything that happens to them comes from God and is wanted by God. Burnt offerings, sacrifices, even human ones, are offered to wheedle some favor from a pitiless god. The Christian God has inherited that terrified worship. "The fear of God is the beginning of wisdom" is not meant to terrorize. Fear of God, an abject fear of God, is never an appropriate approach to Him. If we believe that "God is love" we will have the very best impression of God and religion that it is possible to have on this earth. St. John wrote to his church at Ephesus and said: "There is no fear in love, but perfect love casts out fear; fear has to do with punishment, and whoever fears has not reached perfection in love" (1 John 4:18).

The ministry of La Salettes, lay and religious, has a definite purpose, to invite people to come to God and to the Church, out of love and trust, not out of fear. Their ministry is to cast out fear. They do this by showing people that they themselves are not serving out of fear but out of love – love for God and a deep-seated affection for people. They do this by taking the same tactic the Lady used: a warm, oft-repeated invitation. We underestimate the power of open entreaty. We assume that people know they are invited, know they are welcome and wanted. They do not always know. There is positively nothing in the world quite like being invited, being wanted. All this is part of being loved. The Lady could have gone no further if she had not charmed away the children's fear.

3

I Am Here to Tell You Great News

The Lady appeared; so must the reconciler appear. Making an appearance, being seen, being present to people is part of the ministry of reconciliation. Human reconcilers cannot truly reconcile people, bring them back to God. God alone does that. They are only asked to be there and let people know, by word and deed that they are wanted, loved.

The Lady doesn't live on earth, but by appearing as she did on the mountain she implied that she belonged with and to her people. This temporary visibility is a witness to her constant presence to her people. Whoever would exercise reconciliation is called to presence. Jesus did not recruit his disciples in the synagogue on a solemn feast. He went where they lived and worked. Indeed, he came upon them for the first time and called them while they were at work:

> "As he was walking by the sea of Galilee, he saw two brothers, Simon who is called Peter, and his brother Andrew, casting a net into the sea: they were fishermen. He said to them, 'Come after me, and I will make you fishers of [people]...' He walked along from there and saw two other brothers, James, the son of Zebedee, and his brother John. They were in a boat, with their father Zebedee, mending their nets. He called them and immediately... they fol-

lowed him" (Matt 4:18-22).

Christ came upon them in the midst of their life, and on their ground. God always wants to be part of our daily existence. This is the life we live most of the time.

Our Lady of La Salette appeared to Maximin and Melanie in the rush of their own workaday occupation. They were shepherds doing their shepherd task – they had just finished rounding up their cows, and she appeared to them on their own turf. They worked on the summit of a mountain so she went to the mountain. The reconciler is part of people's daily lives, part of them. They may not know where the local church is and they may swear like parakeets but if the reconciler is present to them they know that God has not abandoned them.

> "All this is from God, who reconciled us to himself through Christ, and has given us the ministry of reconciliation, that is, in Christ God was reconciling the world to himself, not counting their trespasses against them, and entrusting the message of reconciliation to us" (2 Cor 5:18-19).

Reconciliation is the grace of God, God in person who, for a reason known only to God, lavishes the divine on people through other people. Since God always takes the initiative to come to people, the reconciler does the same. He or she is present to people, too. He is a bridge and a bridge is not a bridge until it touches both shores. Through his outstretched arms and heart he touches God and people.

The minister of the Gospel takes a page out of God's book. God does not have initiative: God *is* initiative. God initiates everything. The La Salettes, lay and religious, also use the strategy of initiative. The apparition is itself a splendid initiative. It is outreach ministry straight out of Heaven. Taking their cue from Our Lady of La Salette, La Salettes become outreach people. They become communicating people, because at La Salette, Our Lady's agenda consisted in communicating God's message. And she sent Maximin and Melanie forth to that ministry.

La Salette tells us that it is crucially important to meet people and share with them. The Lady gives the children a mission: to tell "all my people" what she told them. She wants this "great news" to come to all her people because it concerns them. It is what they must be and do to achieve happiness.

Happiness and peace are not reserved solely for the next world but come with the presence of Christ in daily living. Christ cannot be present to a person and not fulfill that person.

When all is said and done, the beautiful Lady wishes the bliss of her Son's presence in people's lives. This is La Salette. Nothing more, nothing less.

That truth is the basic message of La Salette - its only bottom line.

> "The Lady's tone of voice, her manner brought Maximin and Melanie literally running down the ravine to stand next to her. There is an unspoken message here: this is how one approaches children, sinners, people. Clearly, the reconciler cannot dress in light, and he/she is not the Lady. But there is a tone of voice to adopt, a manner, a courtesy and an unthreatening presence. The children stood near their "beautiful Lady" and throughout their lives, never left her."

4

IF MY PEOPLE REFUSE TO SUBMIT

MARY SAID: *"If my people refuse to submit, I will be forced to let go the arm of my Son."*

In one and the same sentence she calls us sinners ("will not submit") as well as "my people." We can simultaneously be sinners and yet still be loved by God.

The discourse begins with the declaration that these people are "my people"... What is affirmed here is a mutual belonging. It is, by itself, an affectionate phrase. In spite of all the wrong they are doing, she has to reproach them, because they are still her people. The unstated fact in the message is that she is here, appearing on earth *because* we are, in fact, her people. Disobedience to the will of God is the comprehensive, all encompassing evil they are guilty of. The rest of the message is an itemized list of violations of the law of the Lord. Submission here, of course, means submission to the will of God.

This will of God is always a factor in the existence of a Christian. It is always associated with his or her life. No part of the Christian faith has been more profoundly misunderstood than this truth, that God has a will for each one of us. God wants the people to do certain things and avoid others. But this is not the only point in question here.

What could go unnoticed, unheeded for a lifetime is the reason for the will of God. Is God pleased when we accomplish God's will? Is God pleased when we show the world that God is God, Lord and Master of all, by insisting that all beings perform God's will in all areas of life? Is this part of some divine hang-up that will not allow God to rest until everything and everyone pays tribute to the Godhead?

Surely, God is pleased. But we still must believe that if God's will is not accomplished on a given day God will survive the catastrophe. God's divine existence is not predicated on the acts and attitudes of people. God did very well without me before I came on the scene and will do equally well after I leave it. What I must remember is that God's will for me is not a whim. It is inspired by the Divine desire to see me live the best possible life here on earth. I have to believe – and this is a vital aspect of my faith in God – that God wants me to have all the happiness possible. God's will for me is simplicity itself. Irenaeus said it so eloquently: "The will of God is humanity fully alive." We will begin to understand Our Lady's tears at La Salette when we ponder Irenaeus' statement.

In the end, the *only* thing God wants from me is my own happiness. God only acts out of love for me. The only way I can offend God is by acting against my own welfare, my own happiness and fulfillment. A sin – any sin – is an act or an attitude that violates God's agenda for God's own glory and my own wellbeing and the two always coexist. Truly, the glory of God is man and woman fully alive. The profound sadness of Mary's tears at La Salette comes from her people's complete misunderstanding or misreading of God's intention for them. She would want them as happy and as much at peace as her Son had been when he lived on earth. That the Lady can weep while bathed in the heavenly light of beatitude shows the bottomless depth of her pain.

Christ on the cross did not die for our sins – he died for us. Likewise, Mary at La Salette did not weep for our sins – she wept for us.

Her Son's complete fulfillment on earth always accompanied a persistent concern for his Father's will in every detail of his life. The disciples once returned from a neighboring town where they had bought provisions and "were surprised that Jesus was speaking with a woman." No one dared ask him why he was speaking with a woman but they did urge him to eat something. But he said to them: "I have food to eat of which you do not know."

This is one example of John's question and answer techniques, where one party is referring to material, physical things while Christ has spiritual truths in mind. They do not understand his refusal to eat until he tells them: "Doing the will of him who sent me and bringing his work to completion is my food." Part of the beauty and difficulty of believing consists in trusting that what God wills for me is meant for my good and ultimate happiness. This is not always easy to believe in daily life.

Christ compares accomplishing his Father's will with something as necessary, as life-giving as *food*. He might also have said: "Doing my Father's will is my life." It is interesting to note that Christ does not consider doing the Father's will as anything else but eating food, as nourishment. In his eyes, it may be a task but a rewarding one, even an enjoyable one, since eating is usually a pleasant experience. In this instance, bringing the Samaritan woman back to

God is his food. Restoring the woman to happiness is his purpose in life. "If my people will not submit" is an essential part of the Christian message. It is not a "La Salette original." What is original here is that Our Lady wept over the disobedience of her people. She points to it as the root cause of all evil and unhappiness.

Our Lady of La Salette's concern appears sharp and clear in the words of Christ. His Father's will is a definite and crucial (literally) reality in his life. The words, "If my people will not submit," define that reality in the lives of all people.

THE SINS MENTIONED AT LA SALETTE are not what we today consider *hot sin*. They are not sins of passion, of anger, murder, adultery and all the other vices commonly associated with violence, sensuality and greed. We are taken aback by the apparent dullness and innocuousness of the sins the Lady reproaches her  people. After all, how much harm can violating Sunday rest cause? Is taking the Name of Jesus in vain the equal of murder and adultery? Isn't this sin committed with some degree of inattention and levity? Can omitting prayer cause all that much harm in the world?

We recall that the commandments concerning God came first in the Decalogue and these are the ones La Salette brings to our attention.

When the Lady says that her Son's arm "is so strong and so heavy" that she can no longer restrain it, she is speaking about the weight and the press of sin. But which sin? The ones she refers to later in her message as being "the two things which make my Son's arm so heavy," namely the violation of the seventh day and abusing the Name of her Son.

It might be right to think of these sins as the root cause of all the others. When respect for God is gone, it follows with the certainty of ocean tides that respect for people likewise disappears.

Perhaps had the Lady excoriated the world with scathing admonitions against sins of lust, murder and greed, coupled with absolutely horrifying decimation and destruction of continents, people might have taken notice. But obeying the first, second, and third commandments is altogether too blah and easy even to give it a second thought.

There is a story in the second book of Kings that underscores this kind of selective obedience.

This man Naaman was a clever general in the army of Syria and was in the good graces of his king. But he had leprosy. He learned of a prophet in the land of Israel who could cure him. So he came to Israel with a huge retinue and a letter from his king.

> "The prophet Elisha sent a messenger to him saying, "Go, wash in the Jordan seven times and your flesh shall be restored and you shall be clean." But Naaman became angry and went away saying, "I thought that for me he would surely come out, and stand and call on the name of the Lord his God, and would wave his hand over the spot, and cure the leprosy...." He turned and went away in a rage. But his servants approached him and said to him, "Father, if the prophet had commanded you to do something difficult, would you not have done it? How much more, when all he said to you was, 'Wash and be clean'?" So he went down and immersed himself seven times in the Jordan, according to the word of

the man of God; his flesh was restored like the flesh of a young boy, and he was clean" (2 Kgs 5:10-14).

The importance of honoring the Lord's Day and his Name are strongly highlighted in the apparition. The Lady prefaced her whole message by saying that she had *great news*. In the context of that message, submission means precisely adhering to those very first commandments. In the eyes of God, they are supremely important. They may not impress us but then, God's thoughts are not our thoughts.

In short, because we have come to view the second and third commandments of God as less contemporary and not of *top shelf* importance, does not mean that God views them in that same way. Apparently not, since they rate a full-fledged apparition.

5

It is Strong, Heavy

Mary said: *"It is so strong, so heavy, I can no longer hold it back."*

No one can speak or write about La Salette without speaking about the wrath of God and punishment for sins. The message of Our Lady is incomplete without it. We have noted that fire and brimstone have gone out of sermons and homilies. To blue-pencil these out of a comment on the discourse would be dishonest and misleading.

We know that sin is an offense against God. We also know that sin is offense and injury to the human person. One cannot offend God without injuring oneself as well as others. The injury is not always or immediately visible but neither is cancer. We all know that life and love are difficult, even with the help of discipline. Without it, they are impossible. We all know that dreams are necessary and that they are unattainable without help. Unappealing as it can be, distasteful as it is, correction by God for our erring ways is essential to our dreams. In the end, we would not love a sentimental, wimpy, overly permissive God who would allow us all our ways and all our whims. We would then be forever imprisoned in mediocrity, unable to go beyond today's goodness to tomorrow's excellence and perfection, forever prevented from coming to any fulfillment and within sight of a dream. In fact, we could look upon correction by God as an act of kindness and mercy and of supreme concern. The young child who always lives in a permissive cocoon knows instinctively that he is not loved, that no one really cares.

We know that God does everything out of love. God cannot correct out of hatred, for then God would be betraying and denying God's own self because "God is love." It is typically human and understandably so, to sing of the incident of the land of Coin in polyphonic strains as a paean to God's concerned and watchful love. Conversely, we consider it strange and oddly mysterious – and old style nineteenth century spirituality to boot – that the Lady should speak of famine and re-straining her Son's arm. We must believe that both, God's chas-tisements as well as God's rewards, are signs of God's love. Both threat and promise of La Salette come from the same loving Lord who manifests no lesser love in the than in the other.

In his poem, *The Hound of Heaven*, Francis Thompson writes of God who pursues him like a hound. Life teaches the poet that the Hound is pursuing him to rescue him, not to destroy him. Had the Hound not pursued him and "caught" him he would never have seen God:

> "How little worthy of love thou art!
> Whom wilt thou find to love ignoble thee,
> Save Me, save only Me?
> All which I took from thee I did but take,

Not for thy harms,
But just that thou might'st seek it in My arms.
All of which thy child's mistake
Fancies as lost, I have stored for thee at home:
Rise, clasp my hand and come!"

Martin Luther once said: "Ah, God, punish us, we pray Thee...but be not silent...toward us" (*Table Talk*, LXXXIII).

God punishes but God is not silent. God speaks to us in the Scriptures. God still manifests watchful presence over us by sending God's Mother to reveal God's concern, sorrow, as well as God's life- saving punishments.

The God of Scripture is not a wan, bland, white-bread God. God's love is warm, tender but vigorous. God wants what is best for the people, whether they be individuals or nations. The love affair between Israel and Yahweh seesawed throughout the Hebrew Bible, the New Testament and continues to do so today. The Prophet Hosea perhaps best expressed this off-and-on state of affairs when he wrote:

> "When Israel was a child I loved him, out of Egypt
> I called my son. The more I called them, the farther
> they went from me, sacrificing to the Baals and
> burning incense to idols. Yet it was I who taught
> Ephraim to walk, who took them in my arms; ...
> drew them with human cords, with bands of love;
> fostered them like one who raises... an infant to his
> cheeks; I bent down to feed them" (Hos 11:1-4).

THE LORD LOOKS UPON US AS INDIVIDUALS AND AS NATIONS. He looks upon us as a parish and also as a Church.

The teaching of the Communion of Saints is slowly, ever so slowly, becoming popular again. Solidarity is in the air. Our union as one people under God is more than a slogan. It is a reality, sometimes grim sometimes grand, depending on reward or punishment.

This Communion of Saints is a sublime phenomenon that makes a whole group or church, or world better because one person within it is holy. The uprightness, the righteousness of the individual sanctifies the whole community. *This improvement* is not calculated like the mathematical average of the group, as, for example, the coming of a ninety-year-old person in a high school class would raise the average age of the class. This kind of average would in no way influence or improve or affect the individual within the class. But the Communion of Saints brings about, in a mysterious, grace-filled way, a raising of individual holiness through that one holy person.

Pope Saint John Paul II

The reality of the Communion of Saints has a grim side, too. The more sin there is in a community, the more the individuals who form that community share its evil. In short, there is a Communion of Saints as well as a Communion of Sin. We share our neighbor's unrighteousness and evil. Solidarity is a two-edged sword. The world is better for a Mother Theresa of Calcutta and worse for a person who sees a poor neighbor and does nothing. Just as the good gathers together those who practice it and leads them to the solidarity of a true communion, so the evil locks them into its prison where there is only the appearance of communion which is really a type of complicity.

In one of the most original passages of his *Exhortation on Reconciliation*, Pope Saint John Paul II assesses personal responsibility within the realm of social sin. Without ascribing unwarranted guilt to individuals for evils before which they stand helpless, he recalls the consequences suffered by society as a result of compromises and passive complicity.

> "To speak of social sin means in the first place to recognize that, by virtue of human solidarity which is as mysterious and intangible as it is real and concrete, each individual's sin in some way affects others. This is the other aspect of that solidarity which on the religious level is developed in the profound and magnificent mystery of the communion of saints, thanks to which it has been possible to say that "every soul that rises above itself, raises up the world" (4)

To this law of ascent there unfortunately corresponds the law of descent.

> "Consequently one can speak of a communion of sin, whereby a soul that lowers itself through sin drags down with itself the church and, in some way, the whole world. In other words, there is no sin, not even the most intimate and secret one, the most strictly individual one, that exclusively concerns the person committing it. With a greater or lesser violence, with greater or lesser harm, every sin has repercussions on the entire ecclesial body and the whole human family. According to this first meaning of the term, every sin can undoubtedly be considered as social sin.

> "Some sins, however, by their very matter constitute

a direct attack on one's neighbor and, more exactly, in the language of the Gospel, against one's brother or sister. They are an offense against God because they are offenses against one's neighbor. These sins are usually called social sins, and this is the second meaning of the term. In this sense, social sin is sin against love of neighbor, and in the law of Christ it is all the more serious in that it involves the Second Commandment, which is "like unto the first."

"Likewise, the term social applies to every sin against justice in interpersonal relationships, committed either by the individual against the community or by the community against the individual. Also, social is every sin against the rights of the human person, beginning with the right to life and including the life of the unborn or against a person's physical integrity. Likewise social is every sin against others' freedom, especially against the supreme freedom to believe in God and adore him; social is every sin against the dignity and honor of one's neighbor" (5).

THERE IS No DOUBT that the Lady of La Salette referred to the existence of social sin. The individual, personal sins existed in 1846 also, because each cart-driver who used the name of her Son, each person who worked on Sunday and did not go to Mass offended God personally. Why then should God punish society for the sins of individuals? The reasons cited above and in the Pope's message would involve the influence of the individual's conduct, good or bad, on the community as a whole. We might suggest that in cases such as those mentioned at La Salette (missing Mass and/or working on Sunday, using the name of Christ in vain, avoiding penance), the practices had become so widespread that individual correction would prove futile. The evil had become endemic. All her people had been affected by it.

It had also been long lasting. The punishment was not to be meted out because of a few brief incursions into evil. The Lady said:

"How long a time I have suffered for you! If my Son is not to abandon you, I am obliged to plead with him without ceasing."

To counter the evil mounting to heaven like an obscene cloud, the Lady had to resort to constant, unrelenting entreaty before God.

As the Lady speaks, one senses a sorrow beyond that of tears. There is a deep-seated grief at having to punish, to inflict pain upon her people. First, the entire threat of punishment is made conditional.

"If my people refuse to submit... If I want my Son not to abandon you."

Then, reasons for the coming punishment are amply provided. The people must be made to see that the punishment fits the crime: the violation of the law of Sunday rest; blasphemy; omission of Mass; absence of penance. The Lady adds that these corrective measures are long overdue: the arm of her Son has become...

...so strong, so heavy, that I can no longer hold it back... How long a time have I suffered for you... However much you pray, however much you do, you will never be able to recompense the pains I have taken for you. This (working on Sunday) is what makes the arm of my Son so heavy.

One cannot avoid noting how hesitantly God punishes... when it has come to that.

6

How Long a Time

Mary said: *"I Have Suffered for You..."*

The subject of suffering always brings people down to Monday morning reality. The reconciler's task consists in praying, greeting people, establishing a relationship... and suffering.

Why this is so is a mystery, just as suffering is a mystery. The only reason we can offer is that Jesus himself suffered for the sins of humankind. He suffered harassment from those who were jealous of his ministry, he suffered at Gethsemane and he endured death on the cross. Suffering played a large part in his life. The first Reconciler thus made a bold statement: he came to rescue humankind from sin and he did it out of love, in the power of God and through suffering. Suffering is not popular. Mere mention of it is commonly avoided. We rarely, if ever, read of it in Catholic publications or hear about it from the pulpit. At La Salette, Mary brings it to the fore as the principal means of protecting her people from punishment. This reconciliation ministry is only for those who love God and people enough to suffer for them and with them. The mention of suffering in Mary's discourse is bold indeed: the Mother of God is suffering in the very heart of glory. Who could have imagined it if she had not clearly stated it?

Suffering is an integral part of the ministry of reconciliation. Even in heaven. The reconciling person, following in the footsteps of the reconciling Christ and his reconciling Mother will undergo suffering for the reconciliation of all people. All reconcilers are acquainted with suffering. It is part of the charism of reconciliation. Why this is so is a mystery, just as the tears of the Lady are a mystery, just as the suffering Christ and the Cross are a mystery.

Still, there are some visible, appreciable reasons for joining reconciliation with suffering:

> a) Suffering is a sincere and powerful proof of love. It is a crucible where true affection is tested. We have all heard of fair weather friends who desert their "loved" ones when the sun stops shining and hailstones begin to fly. Somewhere Pascal wrote: "I believe a witness who is strangled for his faith." More than any other sentence, Our Lady's revelation of suffering for us is the most important declaration of love in the entire message of La Salette. Those words, accompanied by her tears are the most felt expression of God's concern for us in modern times.

> b) Suffering is the most powerful sign of faithful,

abiding love the Lady manifested at La Salette. "How *long* a time have I suffered for you!.. I am obliged to plead with him without *ceasing*. However much you pray, however much you do, you will never recompense the pains I have taken for you."

c) Again, the tears – the most striking and visible of all the symbolic gestures the Lady has given – are an obvious sign of suffering. They manifest a surfeit of moral pain. It was important to the Lady that these tears be *seen*. When the children first see her, she is sitting on the stone, her face in her hands, in an obvious expression of sorrow. In fact, this vision of the weeping Mother came before her spoken word. She allowed the children to see her thus afflicted and the scene was set. The tears clearly became the main theme, the message and the mood of the apparition.

d) The crucifix, which seemed alive to the children, is another open recall of suffering. It *connects* Calvary with the entire message. This suffering Person on the cross is her Son and she is suffering with him. The tears falling over the cross seem to point to that compassion. The crucifix also recalls the saving act of Calvary and the redeeming power of all suffering endured in union with him and in his name.

e) This aspect of suffering is also the most forbidding element in the La Salette event. People instinctively recoil from pain, any pain. When Jesus first told his disciples of his coming Passion, "that he must go to Jerusalem and suffer greatly from the elders, the chief priests, and the scribes, and be killed..." Peter took him aside and began to rebuke him, "God forbid, Lord! No such thing shall ever happen to you."

What Jesus said and did next is revealing. "He turned and said to Peter, 'Get behind me, Satan! You are an obstacle to me. You are thinking not as God does, but as human beings do" (Mat 16:21-23). There is no doubt that the Lord hated suffering, as the agony in the garden shows. But it was important that he not use his divine power to escape suffering and death. It was crucial (literally) that he not be prevented from showing his love for humankind by "going the limit" for it. In view of this, anyone who would keep the Lord from suffering and this manner of expressing love is acting in the name of Satan. Peter discovers this when the kindly Jesus calls his friend Satan.

The Apostles show their aversion to suffering, especially to the specter of a suffering Christ when the Master predicts his Passion for the second time. "As they were gathering in Galilee, Jesus said to them, 'The Son of Man is to be handed over to men, and they will kill him, and he will be raised on the third day.' And they were overwhelmed with grief" (Mat 17:22-23).

f) Suffering is also La Salette's most difficult obstacle. The apparition has never inherited the appealing image of Lourdes and Fatima. It was never meant to. La Salette has espoused the central message of the Gospel, salvation, redemption, and love through suffering. Tears and suffering are shown as signs and symbols of concern. The problem is that suffering is explicitly mentioned by the Lady and powerfully projected on all the world's screen by her sorrowful, sitting posture and her tears. People are touched by the statues and paintings of La Salette. They are sympathetic as anyone would be in the presence of a weeping adult at a wake. Especially when the adult is the Virgin. The immediate temptation is to sentimentality. But actual sharing of suffering and sorrow is another matter.

For this reason, La Salette will never be self-propelled. The first years after the apparition witnessed a widespread, spontaneous publicity. It was new, interesting, striking. It leaped oceans and continents. But La Salette will never have the Lourdes appeal, with the young, white-dressed and smiling Virgin, the miracles, the lovable and canonized Bernadette Soubirous. Nor will it ever be a Fatima with the dancing sun and the saintly children.

La Salette has to be literally, almost physically, taken to all nations and peoples. La Salette is unique in the Gospel harshness of its message. It is alone in the Virgin's end-of-message insistence on disseminating the message. "Well, my children, you will make this known to all my people." This command was repeated by the Virgin, but with this singular stress which can only be given in French (she had reverted from the native Patois to French for this last word): "Vous le ferez bien passer a tout mon peuple"; which could be loosely translated, if at all, with "Well, my children, *make sure* you make this known to all my people."

La Salette is a "witness message." It is prophetic. It is reproachful, accusing and threatening – not the stuff of popularity. In this it has inherited some of the hard, challenging character of the gospel. Whoever preaches it will be forever compared to the message and measured against it.

The charism of La Salette contains the elements of pain and proclamation. It includes the element of witness. They who preach suffering for the sake of the salvation of others, must have suffered, or be willing to suffer in the same way. Those who preach prayer and penance must also be prayerful and penitential people. Those who preach the tears must have cared enough, must be concerned enough about people to weep for them.

Speaking to church crowds about suffering in these times of instant and full gratification is not the most appealing prospect. I have often found myself ducking the suffering theme in homilies and conferences by quickly shifting gears to the splendors of love in St. John and the necessity of prayer. Beautiful topics in themselves and splendid enough to make me forget, for the moment, that I have neatly sidestepped that element that accompanies love and prayer to purify them. Down deep, where conscience sometimes slumbers, I know better.

It is often said that it is impossible to bear something for someone else. Is that true? In Jocelyn Gibb's *Light on C. S. Lewis*, Nevill Coghill tells a story C. S. Lewis once told him.

> "Lewis married late in life. In his marriage he found the very perfection of love, but too soon the wife he loved so much died of cancer. Once when Lewis was with Coghill he looked across the quadrangle at his wife, 'I never expected,' he said, 'to have in my sixties the happiness that passed me by in my twenties.' 'It was then,' writes Nevill Coghill, 'that he told me of having been allowed to accept her pain.' 'You mean,' said Coghill, 'that the pain left her, and that you felt it for her in your body?' 'Yes,' said C.S. Lewis, 'in my legs. It was crippling. But it relieved hers.'"

The Beatitude says, "Blessed are the merciful." The Hebrew word for mercy is *Chesedh*. In his commentary on Matthew, T. H. Robinson writes of this word: "*Chesedh* is the perfection of that mystical relation of one personality to another which is the highest of all possible grades of friendship. It means a systematic appreciation of other persons, the power, not merely to concentrate blindly on them, but to feel deliberately with them, to see life from their point of view."

It is involvement so complete that it issues in self-identification with the other person. It was this involvement and this self-identification that God accepted in Jesus Christ in the Incarnation. Matthew (8:17) quotes Isaiah 53:4: "This was to fulfill what was spoken by the prophet Isaiah: 'He took our infirmities and bore our diseases.'" There is a real sense in which Jesus Christ bore and endured the sin and the suffering of the human situation; and those who are his followers must be like him (6).

Simone Weil, in her *Waiting for God*, wrote:

"It is in affliction itself that the splendor of God's mercy shines, from its very depths, In the heart or its inconsolable bitterness. If still persevering in our love, we full to the point where the soul cannot keep back the cry, 'My God, why hast thou forsaken me?' If we remain at this point without ceasing to love, we end by touching something that Is not affliction, not joy, something that is the central essence, necessary and pure, something not of the senses, common to joy and sorrow: the very love of God.

"We know then that joy is the sweetness of contact with the love of God, that affliction is the wound of this same contact when it is painful, and that only the contact matters, not the manner of it.

"It is the same as when we see someone very dear to us after a long absence; the words we exchange with him do not matter, but only the sound of his voice, which assures us of his presence.

"The knowledge of this presence of God does not afford consolation; it takes nothing from the fearful bitterness of affliction; nor does it heal the mutilation of the soul. But we know quite certainly that God's love for us is the very substance of this bitterness and this mutilation."

7

I Plead Without Ceasing

MARY SAID: *"If I want my Son not to abandon you, I am obliged to plead with him without ceasing."*

The reconciling person has to be ready for the long haul. Reconciliation is never a one-time event. It is a never-ending process. We are always being reconciled. One day at a time. On a rare occasion the reconciler will witness a sudden conversion. This is a consolation and it is bound to be a rare one—however it is still part of a long process.

"Abandon" is radical, terminal speech. It is all the more severe when we realize that it goes against every word and promise of the entire Bible. The New Testament, especially, is held together by Christ's insistence that he is the Emmanuel, God with us, (Matt 1:23), that he is present wherever two or three are gathered in his name, (Matt 18:20), and that he will be with his Church until the end of time, (Matt 28:20). By using the threat of abandonment, the Lady went to the limits of the vocabulary of punishment. Nothing else could be said. The word says reams about the seriousness of the offenses mentioned in the apparition.

Her people's estrangement from God prompts Mary to say that she prays *without ceasing* for her people. Actually, two elements stand out here: her fidelity and her prayer.

This quality of fidelity is essential to the reconciler. Earlier, the Lady had said, *"Long have I suffered for you..."* Now she adds, "I am obliged to entreat him *without ceasing."* She has had vast experience in this intercession—reconciliation ministry. It is clear, too, from her discourse that the evils she denounced are still with us.

A reconciler has this attractive "I'll-stay-by-you" quality and cultivates it. Reconciliation has to do with people, with relationships. A relationship has to have some degree of peace and pleasantness to be acceptable. The participants should be able to talk with one another – and allow the other(s) to talk. The largest part of a relationship, it would seem, is a listening heart.

Confidence stems from God. This is faith and it is a gift. But in the present economy of things God has become flesh, incarnate, in the Church and in people. And so, gloriously and sometimes tragically, confidence in religion also rests with the people who are its ministers or who, in the mind of all, speak in its name. Whether he 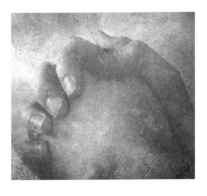 knows it or not, at any given moment, the face of the reconciler is the face of the Church and the reconciler's action becomes the Church's. Anyone performing the service of reconciliation is saying: "You can trust me. I will stand by you in prayer as well as in daily life." He is humanly loyal and faithful because reconciliation is not a one-act play. It is more often a life-long drama strewn with glory and pain... A reconciler is friend, which means that he has acquired the ability to walk with people for the time, brief or long, that the reconciling grace brings two people together.

THE PRAYER OF ABRAHAM

The first prayer recorded in the Old Testament is a prayer of intercession – reconciliation offered by Abraham in the book of Genesis. The old Patriarch, a friend of God who could stand before the Lord and pray that the city of Sodom might be spared destruction at God's hands.

We know that Sodom was destroyed, but we also know that if intercession could have saved it, it would have been spared. Abraham used all the skill of an oriental merchant to plea-bargain before the Lord. He appealed to God's justice, assuming that surely God would never want to destroy the just with the unjust. The Bible shows us a God who goes to Sodom "in person" to see whether the residents of Sodom "have done altogether according to the outcry that has come to me; and if not, I will know."

Here Scripture lays out a spectacular, heroic scene for us. We know that the Lord is about to destroy Sodom and the only person able to avert the disaster is Abraham. The men who were his guests leave for Sodom "while Abraham remained standing before the Lord."

Abraham's prayer of intercession reveals his own intimacy with the Lord. He can afford to bargain and "negotiate" with the Lord because Abraham is the friend of God. Abraham wisely began with a question to which he already knew the answer: "Will you indeed sweep the righteous with the wicked? Suppose there are fifty righteous within the city; will you then sweep away the place and not forgive it for the fifty righteous who are in it?"

Abraham wanted to save the city of Sodom. Taking full advantage of his friendship with Yahweh he brought down the number of just people that will cause the Lord to relent and save the city. He daringly progressed from fifty to forty-five to forty, then to thirty and to twenty. The old patriarch even brought the number down to ten and the Lord said, "For the sake of ten I will not destroy it."

It's more than a charming scene. It's an outright invitation to intercede for people we love and who need intercession. We cannot forget that this is Scripture's first prayer. God went as far as God possibly could with Abraham's prayer until the Patriarch himself saw fit to cease and desist for fear of mocking God. It is Abraham, not God, who ends the pleading.

Abraham's intercession and Mary's at La Salette have a few things in common:

1) Both intercessions are made *in favor of people* to save them from punishment. This focuses attention on a very important point of our relationship with God: Abraham was a friend of God because his life was not just a "me and God" affair. A "me-and-God" exclusive relationship can be selfish, non-committal, uninvolved. God wants me involved and connected with those around me. Mary is such an effective intercessor because her first "yes" was in favor of people: she said yes when she was asked to play a role in the salvation of the world. At La Salette, she was interceding for people, her people.

2) Both intercessions—Mary's and Abraham's—are *persistent*. Abraham goes the limit, so to speak; and Mary intercedes "without ceasing". "How long have I suffered for you!" she says.

3) Abraham's prayer is *bold*: he intercedes fearlessly, almost brazenly, to save the city of Sodom. Thus, all intercession is persistent: it is made primarily in favor of people. And bold. It is always bold.

The old principle that grace builds on nature is played out here in full. The color of reconciliation will take on the color that the reconciling person gives it. If he is unpleasant, unfaithful, unable to undertake and nurture a relationship, he will alienate whoever comes seeking grace. It is part of the very special goodness of God that God wants people to approach through other human beings. In all the universe there is nothing quite like the wonder of seeing one person leading another to peace with himself and with God. Often the odds on the conversion of a particular person are, in human terms, slim. We think of Monica, the mother of St. Augustine, who

prayed twenty years for her son's conversion. It is difficult to imagine that Monica's love and concern for him was not part of the gift of conversion. The reconciler's human loyalty, his faithfulness to God and the person, are flesh and blood reflections of God's own steadfast love. Faith in God and loyalty to people go hand in hand.

Clearly reconciliation (conversion) is a gift from God. But it is given very often through the service of a human person who reflects God and the grace. We often call him or her a reconciler. It is, of course, a manner of speaking. God alone reconciles. God reconciles people to God's own self. God never needs to be reconciled to anyone. But God chooses to share the wonder of reconciliation with another human being. The reconciling person becomes the Lord's eyes and hands and heart.

To be used by God to bring about a radical change, a conversion of mind and soul of the neighbor is to be given a share in the work of the Cross. It is an extraordinary gift. The reconciler becomes a part of the reconciling grace given to God's people. He or she becomes a grace with a face.

8

You Will Never Repay

Mary Said: *"However much you pray, however much you do, you will never be able to recompense the pains I have taken for you."*

***Moses*, the statue by Michelangelo**

No prayer or deed can reward the Lady's long-lasting intercession on our behalf. This is a clear reproach. It is also a clear declaration of our worth in her eyes. She values us, her people, so much that nothing can compensate for the immense pains she has taken for us. There is fidelity here. There is intense effort, endless exertion in our favor.

This is indeed a formidable assertion. All the world's peoples and all their good deeds and all their prayers could not reach the power and remunerate the suffering she has endured for them.

What the Lady does so we also are urged to do. If she interceded for us, so are we to pray for ourselves and for one another. Her words are not for our hearing only but for our emulation and imitation.

Her intercession is crucial. Because of it Christ has not abandoned his people. The intercessory element in La Salette is prominent. Earlier she had said: "If I want my Son not to abandon you, I am obliged–note the strong word–*to plead* with him without ceasing."

The Prayer of Moses

The first prayer offered in the Bible was a prayer of intercession and it came at a dramatic moment. The Israelites saw that Moses delayed coming down the mountain, so they fashioned a golden calf and decided to make it their god.

> The Lord said to Moses: "Go down at once! Your people whom you brought up out of the land of Egypt, have acted perversely; they have been quick to turn aside from the way that I commanded them: they have cast for themselves an image of a calf, and have worshiped it and sacrificed to it, and said, 'These are your gods, O Israel, who brought you up out of the land of Egypt!' The Lord said to Moses, "I have seen this people, how stiff-necked they are. Now, let me alone, so that my wrath may burn hot against them; and of you I will make a great nation."

> But Moses implored the Lord his God, and said, "O Lord, why does your wrath burn not against your people, whom you brought out of the land of Egypt with great power and with a mighty hand? Why should the Egyptians say, 'It was with evil

intent that he brought them out to kill them in the mountains, and to consume them from the face of the earth'? Turn from your fierce wrath: change your mind and do not bring disaster on your people. Remember Abraham, Isaac, and Israel, your servants, how you swore to them by your own self, saying to them, 'I will multiply your descendants like the stars of heaven, and all this land that I have promised I will give to your descendants, and they shall inherit it forever.'" And the Lord changed his mind about the disaster that he planned to bring on his people (Exod 32:7-15).

This is one of the first prayers of the Old Testament and it is clearly an intercessory prayer. The Old Testament never says that prayer is necessary for an ongoing relationship with the Lord but events declare it so.

In this case, the Lord is the first to see what the Israelites are doing while Moses is with him on the mountain. Exodus does not show us a calm and cool God. The vocabulary of anger is wrath 'burning hot', and 'fierce wrath.' This anger will bring 'disaster' on his people. The question Exodus intends to answer is, "How does one go about cooling the anger of God, or even 'changing his mind' as it is clearly said here?

The only way, says Exodus, is intercession, prayer. It is a powerful means since God even makes this plain avowal to Moses: "Now let me alone, so that my wrath may burn hot against and I may consume them." The last sentence in this paragraph has the ring of a holy *bribe* as God says to Moses: "And of you I will make a great nation."

We then see Moses interceding for the people. He reminds God of the ancient patriarchs of the past, Abraham, Isaac and Israel (Jacob). He puts words into the mouths of the Egyptians who would ridicule the Israelites as they tried to convince them that this God lured them into the desert to kill them. Moses further reminds God of God's own promises to make Israel into a great nation and multiplying them "like the stars of heaven."

It is revealing that Exodus doesn't merely say that Moses interceded before God, but includes the prayer of intercession, the words of Moses.

The prayer of Moses is supremely effective and Exodus makes that clear. To make his point, the writer first shows us a fuming God whose wrath is "burning hot" against Israel and is ready to "consume them". After the prayer of Moses we are suddenly told: "the Lord changed his mind about the disaster that he had planned to bring on his people."

Abraham Joshua Heschel tells the story of the young shepherd and scholar:

> There was a young shepherd who was unable to recite the Hebrew prayers. The only way in which he worshiped was "Lord of the world! It is apparent and known unto you, that if you had cattle and gave them to me to tend, though I take wages for tending from all the others, from you I would take nothing, because I love you."

One day a learned man passing by heard the shepherd pronounce his offer and shouted at him: "Fool, do not pray thus." The shepherd asked him: "How should I pray?" Thereupon the learned man taught him the benedictions in order, the recitation of the Shema and the "silent prayer," so that henceforth he would not say what he was accustomed to say.

After the learned man had gone away, the shepherd forgot all that had been taught him, and did not pray. And he was even afraid to say what he had been accustomed to say, since the righteous man had told him not to.

One night the learned man had a dream, and in it he heard a voice: "If you do not tell him to say what he was accustomed to say before you came to him, know that misfortune will overtake you, for you have robbed me of one who belongs to the world to come." At once the learned man went to the shepherd and said to him: "What prayer are you making?" The shepherd answered: "None, for I have forgotten what you taught me, and you forbade me to say 'If you had cattle.'" Then the learned man told him what he had dreamed and added: "Say what you used to say."

"Behold, here is one who had neither Torah nor words; he only had it in his heart to do good, and this was esteemed in heaven, as if this were a great thing. The merciful One desires the Heart. Therefore let men think good thoughts, and let these thoughts be turned to the Holy One, blessed be he" (7).

Prayer is a prominent element
in the message of La Salette

1) The Lady first confesses: "If my Son is not to abandon you, I am obliged to entreat him without ceasing." There are three "extreme" words here that stress prayer as essential to life.

> a) The first extreme word is "abandon." This means forsaking, forswearing, deserting, with a strong note of finality to it.

> b) The second extreme word notes prayer as a serious duty: the Lady is "obliged" to pray. There is no choice. Prayer is a necessity. For the individual as well as for society and the world, it is an obligation. We were reminded how dreadfully serious this duty is. It is a duty assigned to the whole world, because it is within the physical, psychological and spiritual capacity of everyone. Not everyone can go to foreign lands, engage in heavy penance, preach mighty homilies and direct widespread works. But everyone can pray.

Mystics and theologians have been writing for centuries on the rationale for prayer. The truly wondrous verity is that God does not really 'need' our prayer in the same way that we need oxygen to breathe. During the millions of millennia before human life on earth, God did without human prayer. But within the mysterious

God and-me equation there is God's real and incredible yearning for communication with people, a God-created need that God has chosen not to do without. Who will ever understand the deep well-springs of love that have made prayer God's own insatiable need? At La Salette the Lady asks that her people take this need seriously.

> c) "Constantly" ("without ceasing") is the third extreme word here. "Without ceasing" means that it is never possible to pray enough. Even the Lady's own prayer has to be endless.

The principal teaching about prayer in the New Testament is that it be constant, persistent. "Then he told them a parable about the necessity for them to pray always without becoming weary." Then Christ compares the mercy of God with the self-seeking justice of a corrupt judge who protects the widow's rights for fear of her vengeance (Luke 18:1-8).

2) Further into the discourse the Lady asks the children: "Do you say your prayers well, my children?" Maximin answers for both: "Hardly ever, Madame." The Lady replies: "Ah, my children, you should say them well, at night and in the morning, even if you say only an *Our Father* and a *Hail Mary*, when you can't do better. When you can do better, say more."

The Lady places the word "well" into her question as well as into her admonition. Presumably, this would not only mean well said, well formulated or articulated, but also emphacised that their prayers should be said with an attentive heart and with faith—*quality prayer, personal prayer*.

The Lady is a realist. Other humans might have advised them to go far beyond the Lady's requirements. The morning and evening prayer she asked them to say would serve to encompass the entire day and consecrate it to the Lord. The Lady's insistence is not so much on the brevity of the prayer but on its daily offering. Prayer need not be continuous but it must be continual. Two mentions of the importance of the Eucharist should also be included in the Lady's insistence on prayer.

9

I KEPT THE SEVENTH DAY FOR MYSELF

MARY SAID: *"I gave you six days to work;
I kept the seventh for myself, and no one will
give it to me. This is what makes the arm of
my Son so heavy."*

What does the lord mean when when he declares having reserved the seventh to himself? The Lady is obviously not the one who gave us the commandment and reserved the seventh to herself. She is speaking here in the name of God. But what makes the violation of this commandment so serious? The French version says:

> *Je vous ai donne six jours pour travailler, je me suis
> reservé le septième et on ne veut pas me l'accorder.
> C'est ça qui appesantit tant le bras de mon Fils.*
> (see translation in subtitle above)

Why should the violation of this commandment be so serious? Why should this infraction be so crushing? Why wouldn't injustice, immorality, murder, treachery, infidelity, violence of all kinds be more serious than not giving this day to the Lord? Why should working on this particular day be so "deadly"? Why should this be one of the two reasons, practically, for her coming to her to speak to us?

This is undoubtedly a case where the Lord's thoughts are not our thoughts. Is God really altered, will God's happiness and power be forever impaired if I work on Sunday? Will the world suffer or come to an end if I labor on this day? We could go so far as to say, "Is La Salette still relevant today if it highlights such a 'passé' commandment when our entire physical world is being irremediably fouled and destroyed; when people are tortured around the world and whole nations are dying?"

A Special Day for a Special Love

What does it mean actually to give this day to the Lord? Giving a day is only a manner of speaking. What I am really giving is myself... to the Lord, exclusively, on that day. Throughout the week I am busy with my profession, my work, my many obligations, which are all accomplished in the name of the Lord, or course, but not in an exclusive manner.

God does not, in fact, want the day – or any day, be it Sunday or Wednesday. God wants me and wants me exclusively for one whole day in the week. Any lover wants his beloved to himself at special moments and times. This is supremely vital for any love relationship. Without these moments, these special moments, love cannot grow. It cannot even exist. This is a day when everything other than God ceases to exist in the lives of people. In the mind of the Lord, the observance of this day, or its violation, will express the quality and depth of their relationship to God. When this love-tribute is withheld from God, the Lord will make the displeasure known to the loved one – God's people.

This eloquently expresses the charism of La Salette. The love of God that has to be expressed in an exclusive and special manner on this day is the core of the Gospel and of Christian life. This observance may be labeled "a little thing." But aren't the expressions of the deepest love made up of apparently insignificant details? How can a loving relationship be maintained and grow without mutual sharing, speaking, writing, communicating in some manner – any manner? Isn't God expressing intense love for God's own people, for the individual people, by wanting them, all and each one of them, completely and exclusively for one whole day?

There is a special gift given on this day, and a special gift required of all people. Six days are dedicated to work and this work is surely the work of the Lord. But the day he wants for himself he grants as a day of rest, of respite. It is a kindly, gentle and generous reminder that love does not only demand work and toil and sweat and worry. Love also wants the beloved to rest in him, and enjoy himself\herself in him. This day of rest is a memorial to the Lord's wish that men and women should have time to live and breathe and not only to exist and survive. Could it also be a reminder that God loves us not only for the work we do, but also because we are who we are, and for no other reason?

When this *detail* is not observed then all other details become unimportant. Refusing or neglecting to honor the Lord on his day is serious because by doing so I am neglecting love and few things can destroy love more completely than neglect.

We return to the Lady's discourse. Why should this violation make "the weight of my Son's arm be so crushing?" Could it be that the great weight of the arm is a reflection of the great love of the heart? The measure of the offense is the reflected measure of the great affection. There is a saying that only a friend can hurt you. Injustice, immorality, murder, treachery, infidelity, violence have one thing in common: they are all sure and certain symptoms of a complete absence of love in our world.

All the tough elements of La Salette: the tears of the Lady, the abandonment by God, the famine are no lesser signs of love than the incident of the Farm of Coin. They point to the very fact that whatever we do, good and bad, means something to God, and that is a sure sign of consideration and affection. Nothing could be worse than God's indifference before our attitudes and our actions.

10

My Son's Name

Mary said: *"And then those who drive the carts cannot swear without throwing in my Son's name. These are the two things that make the arm of my Son so heavy."*

Someone said that the sweetest word in the entire world is "my name." We use names all day to speak to people, inform people, teach people, and tell them we love them. People invite us to "use my name" to secure good and favorable treatment, and to "call me when you can". There are few more sensitive compliments one can give another than to remember his or her name. And there are fewer more maddening moments than when one remembers a face but has forgotten the name that goes with it.

The Name of God is God's own self. The Hebrew Bible states clearly the commandment to honor the name of God: "You shall not take the name of the Lord, your God, in vain. For the Lord will not leave unpunished him who takes his name in vain" (Deut 5:11).

Here the name to be honored is the Son's. The accusation seems to have a double burden of malice within it. Not only is the name of the Son not honored, it is openly disgraced. Since the name of the Son is the Son himself, then the disrespect is directly flung against

Jesus Christ.

Reconciled in His Name

The charism of La Salette is a factor in the Lady's injunction to reverence the name of her Son. In the Hebrew-Aramaic language that Jesus spoke, his name meant "Yahweh Saves." Reconciliation then, was wrought in his person. It is crucial for every person to know that his or her passport to heaven and to glory was countersigned with the name of Jesus. Abusing his name is an indication of ignorance of the Christian faith.

That God should come to earth, be born in the same flesh we wear is a clear will to form community and initiate intimacy with the human race. That he should be given a name, a human name by which he could be distinguished from other humans is another sign that he took on our humanity completely. We remember with awe that this was the name by which his mother and father knew him, and it was also the name his heavenly Father gave him. The angel said to Joseph: "She will bear a son and you are to name him Jesus, because he will save his people from their sins" (Matt 1:21). The name of Jesus tells who he is and what he will do, what will be his mission. That mission will be totally dedicated to the glory of his Father by the salvation of people.

The whole focus of prayer is centered on this Name. It is, in fact, the Name we give to our faith. It is the leverage of all our prayer. The Name is the one we turn to in sorrow and distress, when we skirt the outer edges of hope. Repeatedly in the Gospels, God the Father is shown offering rescue and wholeness "in the name of Jesus." "And whatever you ask in my name, I will do, so that the Father may be glorified in the Son. If you ask anything of me in my name, I will do it" (John 14:13-14).

Discipleship coupled with the call of Christ to follow him is closely associated with his name. In the time of Christ Jewish students chose the Rabbi who would teach them the Law. They stayed with him until they had learned enough to begin teaching the Law they had learned from the master. It was not that way with Christ. The disciples did not choose him. He, Christ, chose them, to be his disciples. They did not learn the Law but Christ himself. "It was not you who chose me, but I who chose you and appointed you to go and bear fruit that will remain, so that whatever you ask the Father in my name he may give you. This I command you: love one another" (John 15:16-17).

Peter was one of those disciples who followed Christ to the end. He preached Christ, healed the sick and the crippled:

> "In his name this man (the cripple) stands before you healed." But Peter ascribed more than healing to the Name. He assured his hearers that all of salvation is accomplished through it. "There is no salvation through anyone else, nor is there any other name under heaven given to the human race by which we are to be saved" (Acts 4:10,12).

Luke wrote this in the time of the Roman Empire, where salvation was said to be exclusively reserved to the Emperor. The writer makes the point that salvation comes only in the name of Jesus Christ.

The Name of Jesus is always used in the Gospels in relation to reconciliation in its various forms. It could be healing, as above, or approaching God anew, in sorrow and repentance.

> "Because of this (the cross), God greatly exalted him and bestowed on him a name that is above every name, that at the name of Jesus every knee should bend of those in heaven and on earth and under the earth, and every tongue confess that Jesus Christ is Lord, to the glory of God the Father" (Phil 2:9-11).

The name that is referred to here by St. Paul is that of "Lord." This is the name above all other names. "It needs to be remembered that in ancient thought a peculiar value was attached to a name. The person himself was supposed to be somehow present in his name, so that in uttering it one brought oneself under the other's influ-

ence. A soldier took his oath in the name of D   Caesar, and thereby became Caesar's man. A Christian convert was baptized in the name of Jesus, and thus yielded himself to Jesus' will and secured his protection. So Paul assumes that the new name bestowed on Christ carried with it an active power, in virtue of which he had a divine authority" (8).

All prophets and preachers have gone forth to preach that Name. Whole civilizations have adopted it and made it their creed and way of life. Generations of emperors and armies have introduced it, supported it and protected it. But no one other than Jesus Christ himself can insure its strength and perseverance. No secular power can long secure its power. No one can give faith, love, justice and peace, except the One who bears the name of Lord, Jesus himself.

Reconciliation is forever and intimately connected with the Name of Jesus. "Thus it is written that the Messiah would suffer and rise from the dead on the third day and that repentance, for the forgiveness of sins, would be preached in his name to all nations" (Luke 24:46-47).

We need not wonder why the Virgin weeps over her Son's offended name. Even were we to concede that this abuse of the Lord's name might be innocent and more casual than culpable, it still evinces a careless approach—to religion and especially to the Person of Christ. Where intimacy is invited, carelessness is in extremely bad, even offensive taste.

By allowing ourselves the liberty of taking "the name of the Lord in vain" we are depriving ourselves of an extremely valuable treasure. We humans need respect and we need someone to respect. We don't know if God fits the description of "hero" but we do need heroes. They are enfleshed ideals and ideals make us look beyond ourselves. In the case of Christ, we have a hero, an ideal, a friend, a lover, a Lord, a God whose total agenda while he was on earth was to gain our freedom and our salvation. His Father sent him to us for this. All that was thus gained, was gained by his kindness, his power and in his Name.

Abusing the name of Jesus means insulting a man, a God who has loved us more than any other person in the world. Far from dishonoring our own name, he has used it to summon us to the service discipleship. God has called us by name.

Honoring the Seventh Day and the Name

At first reading it is difficult to imagine how violations of the law of Sunday rest and disrespect for the name of Christ could be the very sins that prompted this apparition, and that these are the two things that make her task of intercession so extremely painful.

If they could speak out, the churchgoers of any downtown parish would say that there are infinite varieties of thievery that hurt the neighbor—and therefore God—far more. People die of injustices. People suffer from white-collar piracy. Racism, sexism, and all the colors of greed and prejudice certainly deserve a loftier place in the register of vices. Surely, one might imagine, above working on Sunday and using God's name in vain!

And yet, we wonder. The Lady never mentions all those high profile four-star iniquities like adultery, rape, incest, murder, stealing from the poor and burning churches and synagogues She focuses on the eternal truth that God's thoughts are not our thoughts, that whatever comes first with us may not hold first place with Him. Her words in these lines mean that her people need to realign their values and reassess their priorities.

The commandment of Sunday rest has always been one of those ho-hum precepts that can easily serve to flesh out a thin Easter duty confession. People have asked repeatedly why on earth should the Blessed Virgin Mary, the Mother of God, have appeared on earth to tell her people not to work on Sundays.

There must be more to that law than the negative order of abstaining from servile work. Most of the comments and treatises on Sunday celebration underline what the people of God cannot and must not do instead of the positive injunction of leisure in his Name.

Leisure time is indeed the spirit of Sunday rest. Leisure as defined by The American Heritage Dictionary is "freedom from time-consuming duties, responsibilities, or activities." St. Thomas Aquinas, who is slowly falling into grace again after having fallen out of it in the sixties and seventies, teaches that leisure is necessary for the practice of religion. Not merely useful, but necessary. One must be regularly freed from the burden of salaried survival in order to think about, reflect on, and ponder the great truths of God, existence, love, life as well as one's life journey. If one is to relate with others in charity and genuine love, one must first be convinced of the beauty and grandeur of love. One has to retreat within oneself to perceive the marvels and the miracles to be found within oneself, the values and qualities within one's own person in order to be able to behold these same wonders in other people. God as Creator and Redeemer is not automatically part of my existence and way of life. This God is given to people but has to be received, assimilated and absorbed into one's life and daily existence. This takes time.

It also means that time has to be taken away from one's usual workaday, wage earning involvements and preoccupations. The *All Other* demands an *All Other* day. This *day* is a weekly retreat into oneself in order to focus on God.

The ubiquitous search for excellence in our times is symptomatic of a dearth of meaning in our lives. What is excellent surpasses the norm. It is planned, thought out, its inherent difficulties foreseen, its fabrication carefully designed and repeatedly tested. In the mind and purpose of God, the life of humans on earth deserves no less sedulous care and attention if it is to have meaning, if it is to be of any consequence.

We think of religion as a comprehensive whole, as a phenomenon of relationship to God. It also includes the crucial duty of one's relationship with other humans. The worship and service of God, the love of God, placing one's whole life within the confines of God's will: all of this needs reflection, contemplation.

Our association with other people highlights relationships, our capacity to enter into them, grow with them and conserve them. It involves love of self and love of others; service for others, compassion, justice, love, patience, forgiveness: all these things need the same reflection and contemplation, because religion always stands or falls according to the meaning God and others possess within our own lives. This takes time.

It is also revealing to note the Lord's insistence on the Sabbath's being for people and not people for the Sabbath. Sunday rest, or "Day of the Lord," if one thinks well on it, is meant more for humans than for the Lord. Does the Lord need one special day? All days and seasons are his. The need is a human need for leisure—to rest and reflect on the enormous gifts we have received. To think of his goodness to us and to exploit the many gifts he has lavished upon his people. It is meant to be a day when we can enjoy the beauty of earth and sky as well as the gift of the neighbor. This also takes time, quality time.

You shall not take the name of the LORD your God in vain

11

You Pay No Heed

Mary said: *"If the harvest is ruined, It is only on account of yourselves. I warned you last year with the potatoes. You paid no heed. Instead, when you found the potatoes spoiled, you swore, and threw in my Son's name. They are going to continue to spoil, and by Christmas this year there will be none left.*

"Don't you understand, my children? Let me find another way to say it. If you have wheat, you must not sow it. Anything you sow the vermin will eat, and whatever does grow will fall into dust when you thresh it.

"A great famine is coming. Before the famine comes, children under seven will be seized with trembling and die in the arms of the persons who hold them. The rest will do penance through the famine. The walnuts will become worm-eaten; the grapes will rot."

"You pay no heed!" Earlier in her discourse, the Lady had said: "How long have I suffered for you! If my Son is not to abandon you, I am obliged to entreat him without ceasing. And as for you, you pay no heed!

Nine-tenths of the world is filled with nice people. The rest make the evening news. The sins that the Lady condemns are not sins of white-hot malice, or fervent forays into lewdness, lasciviousness, lechery and lust. The evils mentioned at La Salette are attributable to carelessness, indifference. Somewhere in her *Autobiography*, St. Theresa of the Child Jesus writes that she would rather be hated than ignored. Hatred at least takes note of you, notices you. There is no experience quite like being forgotten, omitted, taken for granted, disregarded, overlooked, ignored. And then, there is no experience quite like hearing your name pronounced with esteem and care, nothing quite having your "day"—birthday, anniversary of whatever—noted and celebrated.

At La Salette, all this is tantamount to ignoring the living God. And this leads to ignoring the things of God. The best "things" of God are people. There is more harm done by the indifference of good people than by all the evil people of the world, as the well-known saying teaches us. This is also true in matters of faith, love, work and ministry.

ACEDIA—SPIRITUAL INDIFFERENCE

The fathers of the early church who went out into the desert are popularly thought to have been fleeing the evils of civilization. But this is a simplification. They thought of themselves more properly as going out to fight evil. The demons, as well as the angels, were believed to live in the wilderness and there could be confronted and bested in all their horrible destructiveness.

The besetting sin of the desert fathers was *acedia* or *accidie*, tellingly described as the "devil of the noonday sun." Acedia is spiritual boredom, an indifference to matters of religion, or simple laziness. Symeon the New Theologian wrote to his monks, "Do not forget your special tasks and your handicraft to walk about aimlessly and in dissipation and so expose yourselves to the demon of *accidie*." His remark is almost a commentary on the axiom: "Idle hands are the devil's workshop."

The ancient sin of acedia lies at the root of the pastor's refusal to heed the calling to be the instrument of spiritual growth. In 1977 Carlyle Marney, a distinguished Baptist pastor-to-pastors, spoke at the seminary where I serve. I remember him asking our students if they thought after ten years they would still love the Lord Jesus or if instead would have become hand tamed by the gentry. Of course, he would have been exceedingly surprised if any had confessed that probably the latter would be the case, but the fact is that many ordained persons quickly lose a sense of the excitement of the spiritual quest. They succumb to acedia in those forms that are to a degree peculiar to our times, and yet share much with previous centuries of clergy.

Many of us when we think of the sins of the clergy recall the fallen priest in literature, such as the Reverend T. Lawrence Shannon in Tennessee Williams' play, The *Night of the Iguana*. He was a boozer, a wencher, and had lost his faith. Yet, such a person is less a sinner then he is a casualty. American religion is obsessed with the warm sins such as illicit sex and gluttony. Because many of us are Donatists—believing that the validity of the sacrament depends upon the moral character of its minister, which was condemned as a heresy long ago-we become inordinately concerned when the warm sins are committed by the ordained. What we fail to realize is that pastor or priest who succumbs to the sins of passion is fallen in the same manner as a fallen soldier. These are the demons that threaten anyone who sets out upon the path through chaos. Some will lose.

The sins that should concern us far more deeply are those that prevent the ordained from ever exercising their spiritual vocation.

These cold sins truly violate the mission of the pastor to be a symbol, symbol-bearer, and hermeneut. They arise not from an excess of passion, but from a fear of passion. They are the product of a calculated apathy, sustained only by the embers of a dying soul.

Acedia is the root sin of the clergy as spiritual guides. Like a cancer it eats away at our abandonment of the love of God and his

Field of Coin (Terre du Coin)

creation. It takes a number of forms, which have much in common with those of other centuries but also have their own peculiar twist in our times. (9)

"You paid no heed!" Earlier in her Discourse, the Lady had said: "How long have I suffered for you! If my Son is not to abandon you." This is a key passage in the message of La Salette. Here we collide into the unappealing idea of a punishing God, a God who allows such things as famines to happen.

Whoever answers that objection by saying that humans cause their own ills seems to be ducking the issue. After all, couldn't a wise and kind God cut the famine short or eliminate it altogether? In reality, God is neither responsible nor accountable for all of our ills.

This wise and kind God has also chosen to grant freedom and liberty of action to all peoples. This kind of freedom means that all actions have consequences and humans learn how to live with the consequences of their actions. This is what a child is taught at an early age. To deprive humans of those consequences would be to play games with their freedom and ultimately to really deprive them of this freedom.

But who can fully explain God's actions or account for the myriad deeds of God's providence? We read the scenario of the *Terre du Coin (the Farm of Coin)* and we conclude to God's constant vigilance and concern for humans. We take note of the promise of the mounds of wheat and the self-sown potatoes and we sing carols to God's compassion and intone antiphons to God's understanding and fidelity.

Then we recall that this is the selfsame God who can also threaten punishment if people are not faithful to Him. Love, concern, care, kindness, compassion are two-sided coins. All of God's actions come from love because "God is love." God is as incapable of performing a hateful act as of drawing a square circle.

The whole message of La Salette comes under the heading of God's deep affection for people. The apparition itself was prompted by God's constant concern for all peoples.

Love also is a coin with its reverse side. We come to know God and we discover that anyone who loves with such passion and intensity is no plain-vanilla wimp of a God.

Probably the only answer that makes full sense comes from God's own words in Isaiah. They occur in the bright light of a text on conversion and reconciliation:

Seek the Lord while he may be found, call upon him while he is near, let the wicked forsake their way, and the unrighteous their thoughts; let them return to the Lord, that he may have mercy on them, and to our God, for he will abundantly pardon. For my thoughts are not your thoughts, nor are my ways your ways, says the Lord. (Isaiah 55:6-8)

12

IF THEY ARE CONVERTED

MARY SAID: *"If they are converted, rocks and stones will turn into heaps of wheat, and potatoes will be self-sown in the fields."*

The Bible gives an insight into the reason for the corrective discipline God gives the people. "You must realize that the Lord, your God, disciplines you even as a man disciplines his son." (Deut 8:5)

Conversion or reconciliation, as it is so frequently shown and said in both Testaments, remains the condition for intimacy with the Lord. The figure of speech used here by the Lady is clearly exaggerated expression to articulate unspeakable love. Of course, there have never been self-sown potatoes or stones that have become mounds of wheat. But this is divine language using potatoes and stones to describe for people the soaring, wondrous quality of God's affection for his own. The Lady is telling her people that there is nothing on earth that will adequately describe the joy of God at the sight of his people returning to Him. It is as if the Lady were saying, 'God's love for you will be as unreal and as incredible as self-sown potatoes and rocks that become piles of wheat.' A God who performs such miracles is obviously a joyful, dancing God, eager to reward and show how overwhelming is God's presence on earth.

Conversion must indeed have a high priority in God's scale of values if such remarkable results flow from it. Conversion is the only event in a person's life that will bring God to gift the world with such superlative blessings. We can suppose that such conversion, personal reconciliation, will bring about Messianic abundance among all the peoples of the earth. If God's pleasure is shown by the gifts God showers on people, then we can imagine God to be extremely pleased by any attempt at conversion.

RECONCILIATION IN STAINED GLASS

In the Lady Chapel of London's Westminster Cathedral there is a mosaic which tells the story of the miracle at Cana in one simple image: a man is pouring water from one large jug into another; the water leaves the first jug a light sparkling blue and becomes a deep purple before it reaches the lip of the lower jug. Before our eyes, water turns into wine. "This, the first of his signs, Jesus did at Cana in Galilee, and manifested his glory; and his disciples believed in him." (John 2:1-11)

Until noticing this mosaic, it had never occurred to me that this first sign that Jesus gave—a miracle of transformation—is a key to understanding everything in the gospel. Jesus is constantly involved in transformation: water into wine, bread and wine into himself, blind eyes to seeing eyes, withered limbs to working limbs, guilt into forgiveness, strangers into neighbors, enemies into friends, slaves into free people, dead bodies into living bodies, crucifixion into resurrection, sorrow into joy. Nature cannot grow figs from thistles, but God is doing this in our lives all the time. God's constant business in creation is making something out of nothing. As the Portuguese say, 'God writes straight with crooked lines.'(10)

We all know that conversion is a turning around toward God, an acceptance of God as Lord and Savior. It is no less than an acceptance of a God whose overall conduct and behavior toward us has always been one of acceptance. Acceptance is probably one of the most completely comforting words in any language. It means that all the skeletons in-my closet and my closet itself with all of its combinations and padlocks are accepted by a wondrously understanding God. It means that everything that causes me to abhor me with raging passion and thorough loathing, He accepts with a completely astonishing affection. This God sees shining gifts in me that had been trodden under foot for a lifetime and brings them to light and to life.

The following story does not do complete justice to God's ways but it helps to understand how God's acceptance is almost always expressed in the loving embrace of another human being:

One very special Christmas day, little Amy unwrapped a beautiful golden-haired doll given to her by her grandmother. "It's such a pretty dolly," Amy squealed excitedly, hugging her new doll. "Oh, thank you, Grandma!"

Amy played with her new doll most of the day, but toward the end of the day, she put down her golden-haired doll and sought out one of her old dolls. Amy cradled the tattered and dilapidated old doll in her arms. Its hair had come off; its nose was broken; one eye was gone, and an arm and a leg were missing. "Well, well," smiled Grandma, "it looks as though you like that dolly the best." "I like the beautiful doll you gave me, Grandma," said little Amy. "But I love this old doll most, because if I didn't love her, no one else would."

13

Do You Pray Well, My Children?

MARY SAID: *"Do you say your prayers well, my children?" "Hardly ever, Madame," the two shepherds answered candidly. "Ah, my children, you should say them well, at night and in the morning, even if you say only an Our Father and a Hail Mary, when you can't do better. When you can do better, say more."*

The Reconciler is much like a lobor negotiator. He has to be on speaking terms with labor and management. He has to understand the demands of both and respect and be respected by both sides. Ideally, he loves both sides and seeks the greater good of both. Above all, he is a communicator who speaks and is understood by both sides. Speaking only to one of the parties without communicating with the other will eventually ruin all his efforts to arrive at an equitable agreement. The reconciling person speaks to God and to people and loves them both.

No wonder the Lady said it was very important to pray and to do so at night and in the morning." The night and morning specification seeks to place the entire day under the eye and care of the Lord. She said it was very important to do so, not necessarily to do so at length, but it is very important to pray. It is very important to keep in touch with God, to talk to God, to stay and work in God's presence. This is the principal advantage of prayer: it keeps people in God's environment, with God. To be with Christ is the very height of the spiritual life.

The Gospel of Matthew stresses that point. The Gospel begins by featuring the role of Christ as Emmanuel: "And they shall call him Emmanuel" as is written in 1: 23. In fact, nowhere in the Gospel of Matthew, or in any other Gospel, or anywhere else in the New Testament is Christ called Emmanuel. Matthew is careful to give the translation of this word "which means 'God is with us.'" Later on, this same Matthew will quote Christ, "Where two or three are gathered together in my name, there am I in the midst of them." Still further, Matthew ends his Gospel with the solemn mission, "Go therefore, and make disciples of all nations...and behold, I am with you always, until the end of the age." (Mt. 28:19-20)

To be with someone is the opposite of being abandoned, or cast off, by someone. If to be with is the ultimate happiness, joy and wellbeing, then to be abandoned will constitute the refinement of gloom and sorrow: the ultimate in unhappiness. The only way to head this off is to pray. "If my Son is not to abandon you, I am obliged to entreat him without ceasing." At La Salette, prayer is closely linked with the presence of Christ in the life of the Christian. The Virgin shows that it is possible with constant prayer to maintain such a presence in the lives of others who don't pray. But this is done only by persevering, constant, unceasing prayer. The well-known invocation to Our Lady of La Salette is justified: "Our Lady of La Salette, Reconciler of sinners, pray without ceasing for us who have recourse to you."

The reconciler will be a prayerful person. "To walk in the presence of the Lord," says Henri J. M. Nouwen, "means to move forward in life in such a way that all our desires, thoughts and actions are constantly guided by him. When we walk in the Lord's presence, everything we see, hear, touch, or taste reminds us of him. This is what is meant by a prayerful life. It is not a life in which we say many prayers, but a life in which nothing, absolutely nothing, is done, said, or understood independently of him who is the origin and purpose of our existence" (11).

The Lady's concern in her words to the children is clear. She tells them that it is absolutely important to pray, and to pray morning and night, in order to let nothing of the day's activities be emptied of the Lord's presence. This is an important part of the La Salette charism. There is a habit of prayer as there is a habit of indifference, where prayer is delayed, postponed, omitted for a variety of reasons (sometimes good ones). Sorrow and regret for these omissions imperceptibly diminish until finally there is no prayer at all, and no pretense of praying. Losing the habit of prayer can be dangerous if the habit is prolonged.

"For such there is a story, told by Rabbi Israel Friedman, the Rizhiner, about a small Jewish town, far off from the main roads of the land. But it had all the necessary municipal institutions: a bath house, a cemetery, a hospital, and law court; as well as all sorts of craftsmen—tailors, shoemakers, carpenters, and masons. One trade, however, was lacking: there was no watchmaker.

"In the course of years many of the clocks became so annoyingly inaccurate that their owners just decided to let them run down, and ignore them altogether. There were others, however, who maintained that as long as the clocks ran, they should not be abandoned. So they wound their clocks day after day though they knew that they were not accurate. One day the news spread through the town that a watchmaker had arrived, and everyone rushed to him with their clocks. But the only ones he could repair were those that had been kept running—the abandoned clocks had grown too rusty."(12)

Just as Our Lady was *seen* weeping, *seen* entreating her Son, *seen* begging her people to return to Christ, *seen* and *heard* forever suffering for her people, so the reconciler not only thinks and practices prayer in private but must himself *appear* praying and suffering for the people he or she serves. To return to an earlier leitmotif: the Lady appeared, was seen, then she spoke. Words are not necessarily the most effective way of communicating anything. "Saying your prayers" morning and night seems such a, well, childish thing. However, the Lady is not indulging in childishness. Whatever she mentions at La Salette is important for the quality of human life.

Do you remember where you were during the famous blackout of 2003 when over 55 million people in the northeast U.S. and central Canada lost power? Everything stopped: water, heat and electricity. Some small detail—a faulty switch, loose wiring, careless technicians—might have caused it. Sometimes our spiritual life is blacked out by lack of prayer, or unforgiveness, or negligence in Mass attendance. Small matters in themselves, they can be the faulty switch and the loose wiring that *blacks out* our relationship with the Lord.

14

ONLY A FEW ELDERLY... THE REST WORK ON SUNDAYS

Mary said: *"In the summer, only a few elderly women go to Mass. The rest work on Sundays all summer long. In the winter, when they don't know what to do, they go to Mass just to make fun of religion."*

The Lady boldly says hard and harsh words. She speaks like a prophet. A reconciler is a prophet because he speaks the words of God. The wrath of God and punishment were never popular topics. They are still less in vogue today. Theological fashions have dictated that God is a God of love and that his children are punished enough in the course of living their lives that they need no other suffering from him. And yet, what are we to make of so many passages of the Hebrew Bible and of the New Testament? What are we to make of the discourse at La Salette?

Doesn't the charism of the reconciler also identify on this point with that of the prophet? Isn't he committed to preaching the whole message and not only part of it? In the area of homiletics, priests are leery of preaching on difficult subjects, like social justice, penance, suffering, hell and morality in general.

Father William J. Bausch, writes about the devaluation of priests and the priesthood in the post- conciliar era: "...preaching has changed. Very few sermons are heard in the land about the hard aspects of the Christian life and morality. No more thundering sermons about indecent dress or X-rated movies or birth control or the pains of hell. No strong sermons on social justice. Why? Because the priest, sensing his devaluation, doesn't want to alienate, to create any more distance from himself. After all, he needs to be appreciated" (13).

The Lady directs a sorrowful observation toward people who go to Mass "only to laugh at religion." The Mass is clearly on her mind. Earlier, she had told the children: "only a few rather old women go to Mass in the summer." The whole theme of reconciliation that she proclaims needs to be centered on the great reconciling act of Christ: suffering, death, resurrection, the Eucharist. For Roman Catholics, this is a special sacrament. It is central to faith and reflects the life they lead.

It is central also to the charism of La Salette, simply because it is such an integral part of reconciliation. It is interesting to see how people who don't believe in it have come to view it. No one can accuse Reinhold Niebuhr of being partial to the Catholic Church. He was, in fact, a long-time critic of the Church. After his retirement as professor at Union Theological College in New York, a stroke had kept him from the pulpit and forced him to sit in the pew. He wrote:

> I had always believed that the vitality of religion
> after the rise of modern science, which tended to

discredit the legends of religious history, was due to the simple fact that faith in an incomprehensible divine source-of order was an indispensable bearer of the human trust in life, despite the evils of nature and the incongruities of history. But as I became a pew-worshipper rather than a preacher I had some doubts about the ability of us preachers to explicate and symbolize this majesty and mystery. These pulpit-centered churches of ours, without a prominent altar, seemed insufficient. Moreover, in the non-liturgical churches the 'opening exercises'—with a long pastoral prayer which the congregation could not anticipate or join in- seemed inadequate. I came to view the Catholic Mass, in many religious respects, more adequate than our Protestant worship. For the first time I ceased to look at Catholicism as a remnant of medieval culture. I realized that I envied the popular Catholic Mass because the liturgy, for many, expressed the mystery which makes sense out of life always threatened by meaninglessness."(14)

The central prayer of the Church becomes the most powerful means of reconciliation at the reconciler's command. A reconciling person is a praying, Eucharistic person. By definition. Father Jaouen in his book, *A Grace Called La Salette*,(15) has traced the modern devotion to the Eucharist and the rise of world Eucharistic congresses to La Salette.

15

In Lent to the Butcher Shops

Mary said: *"In Lent, they go to the butcher shops like dogs."*

The scene here is of empty churches and crowded butcher shops.

We discover, if we ever needed to, that the speaker here is not about to mince her words. It isn't so much that God is merely displeased at the sight of displaced values in his people. The Lady's expression, "like dogs" would indicate indignant surprise and disgust. Can we say that the Lady is hurt at the sight of her people going to the meat market like dogs?

We are surprised to hear such an expression in the mouth of the beautiful Lady. This is not mellifluous language because her love for people is robust enough to tell them exactly what she sees and thinks.

This going to the butcher shop like dogs is linked to what should be Lenten observance of penance. This is another gospel guideline, an essential tenet for Christian living. And we wonder why people should add penitential acts to a life already well chaperoned by suffering?

The reason is perhaps that the penance initiative prepares one to meet the unwanted and unexpected lashes of life.

Another reason, and one that seems more attractive, is that there can be no love without pain, suffering and the penance of self-giving. To love is to give and one unaccustomed to sharing life and things with another is a poor candidate for any kind of relationships. People we love define our vulnerabilities and are most capable of inflicting pain upon us. Further, to love others, whether we refer to a human family or to a religious community, implies constant and demanding self-giving. The Lady's strong expression of disgust stands out. These are surely the strongest words and the most striking reprimand in her message. Is this therefore the one we are to take most seriously at heart? Is this reluctance to do penance at the core of all the rest of the ills she mentions? Does penance really have a rationale other than the strengthening of love? Is the Lady telling us that there is no viable Christian existence without some form of self-denial? This is the flipside of the coin of love: the stronger and deeper the love, the angrier the rebuke to betrayed affection.

There is one element common to love and anger, and that is fire.

This passage is blunt and earthy. The words are not the type of expression we would lend to the beautiful, gentle Lady. The people she called my people she now compares to animals that live to eat.

There probably is no gentle manner of introducing humans to the idea of penance. It has never been a popular topic. The Lady must be bringing convincing reasons for the almost crude reproach she throws at all her people. The phrase like dogs is clearly meant to impress, to focus attention on this theme of penance. Christian tradition teaches that penance is training, preparation and discipline for life.

Christian life cannot be lived without it. M. Scott Peck, M.D. begins his best-selling book, The Road Less Traveled, with the sentence: "Life is difficult." Any adult person will concur with that statement. The same tradition teaches that it is hard to live a moral, upright life without the ability to sacrifice, to do without even some of the good, clean, permitted things of this world. A Christian unaccustomed to sacrifice, to self-giving, to loss, will be unable to attain fulfillment neither as a Christian nor as a person. It is consistent with the "God's will is man alive" principle that the Lady should speak forcefully in favor of the observance of what were then prescribed penitential practices. Legislation has changed since 1846 but the obligation to do penance is still as much in force as ever.

Without penance, all human dreams of growth, achievement and excellence can be forgotten. This holds even more truth with regard to spiritual advancement. Penance, unpleasant as it is, prepares us for the seamy, distasteful, unappealing aspects of the ideals we are called to. Love is an ideal and the goal of every breathing human being. There can be no authentic love without selfgiving. Penance in its positive form is self-giving. There can be no love without giving up of time, of preferences, of self-righteousness, of opinions, of impatience. To love God and neighbor means to have genuine affection for another, because of who he or she is. This makes absolute and radical demands on our powers of acceptance. No one can undertake the journey of love without having gone through the ongoing and rigorous training of penance—hence the strong language.

Mary at La Salette appears before the world as a penitential person. We believe her when she says she is constantly suffering for us in heaven, however mysterious this suffering may be. We see her weeping throughout the entire discourse. The reason for this apparition, for the tears, for the suffering, can be none other than an authentic affection for her people. She chose to weep because she could not think of a more eloquent sign of grief and love than tears.

The reconciling person is a loving person. Why else would he or she want to bring people back to God? He has to be able to weep over sin because there is nothing sadder in all the world than a person who willfully turns his back on love and true happiness in Christ. In our own times, a reconciler has to show genuine sadness over persons in the grip of any chemical dependency, of the gambling habit, of compulsive sex, of violence. Real sadness has to be felt and expressed also for people whose sole purpose in life is to make it, spend it and enjoy it.

A true reconciler loves people above all else. In the secret of his soul, at least, he will cry over people who are delivering themselves up to misery and sadness, when happiness and wellbeing are within grasp.

Outside the Gospel and Christ, La Salette is the most beautiful expression of love and concern the world has ever known. The Missionary of La Salette reconciler, lay or religious, has to express that love. Our charism consists not only in preaching the message, the words, the history, but also sharing the love, the affection contained in the apparition.

There is a legend concerning Judas Iscariot. Judas, having betrayed Christ for thirty pieces of silver, went out and hanged himself. After this, Judas found himself at the bottom of a dark and dank pit. He lay there on his stomach for a million years. (Since he was in eternity, he experienced "time" in his own peculiar way.) Slowly and painfully he turned himself over on his back and lay in the darkness for another million years.

He then saw, or thought he saw, a faint light miles above him at the mouth of the pit. Something in him drew him towards the light, or was it the light itself that did the drawing? He couldn't tell. With great difficulty, he stood up and began to climb. For years and years he climbed. Often he slipped back and had to wait a century or two to regain his strength to go on. As he climbed, the light grew stronger, and the closer he got to the mouth of the pit, the more Judas drew strength from the light.

Eventually, after many eons, he pulled himself over the edge and, much to his astonishment, he found himself in an Upper Room where a young rabbi was having a meal with his friends. The young rabbi came over to him, helped him to his feet and said, "Judas! Welcome! We've been waiting for you. We couldn't continue the supper without you." (16).

"During Lent they go to the butcher shop like dogs..."

16

WHEAT GONE BAD

Mary said:
**"Have you never seen wheat gone bad,
my children?"** *"No, Madame,"* Maximin
replied, "we never have." **"But you, my
child, must have seen it once, near Coin,
with your papa. The owner of the field
said to your papa, 'Come and see my
spoiled wheat.' The two of you went. You
took two or three ears of wheat in your
hands. You rubbed them, and they crumbled to dust. Then you came back from
Coin. When you were only a half-hour
away from Corps, your papa gave you a
bit of bread and said, 'Well, my son, eat
some bread this year, anyhow. I don't
know who'll be eating any next year if the
wheat continues to spoil like that.'"** *Maximin replied: "It's very true, Madame. Now I
remember it. Until now I didn't."*

No one could possibly have expected Maximin who hardly remembered getting up in the morning, to retain the short conversation of the farm of Coin. The Lady jogged his memory and he recalled the long forgotten incident. The two men and the boy had reason to believe that they had been completely alone in the field that day. At La Salette, the Lady implied that she had been there and had seen everything.

By implication also, she reminds all her people that there is all the more reason to believe that Jesus was there at Coin also. Her apparition is a reminder of the presence of the Lord even in the most trivial events of our lives; which is to say, that in his eyes, no event in any person's life is trivial. The message of this last paragraph of the Lady's discourse is one of God's concerns for the suffering of God's people.

NEARER THAN HANDS AND FEET

If we would keep the presence of God real and vital and living, God must come out of the sky into the world-which is just what he did in Jesus. "The Word became flesh and lived among us." (John 1:14) As Tennyson put it: "Speak to Him thou for He hears, and Spirit with Spirit can meet—Closer is He than breathing, and nearer than hands and feet." (17)

Details are part of caring and caring is no detail. The incident of the farm of Coin is an example of God's and the Lady's manifest concern for people. This caring-clinic stressed details:

"with your papa"

"The owner of the field said to your papa..."

"You took two or three ears of wheat in your hands"

"You rubbed them together and they crumbled to dust"

"Then you came back from Coin..."

"You were no more than a half hour from Corps"

"And your father gave you a piece of bread"

"And said to you: 'Here, my child, eat some bread...'"

The sheer proliferation of details is meant to jump-start Maximin's memory, but it also shows the extent to which the Lord will go to show care and interest, even in the apparently useless and meaningless details of a small child's daily life.

17

MAKE THIS KNOWN

MARY SAID: *"Well, my children, you will make this known to all my people. Well, my children, make this known to all my people."*

The Lady insisted that her message be made known throughout the world. She addressed them specifically: "You will make this known..." The Lady knew that passing on religious truths, especially when they take the form of reprimands, is a harsh task, one needing the strength of true witnesses. The short duration of the apparition was to be the most pleasant experience of their lives. The tough task of spreading her message was to change their lives forever.

There is no doubt that God's confirming presence in their lives helped Maximin and Melanie fulfill their mission. After the apparition their lives were filled with the hard toil and often physical risks of proclaiming its truth. They manifested surprising moral fortitude. Climbing the mountain road to the site of the apparition one day, one gendarme seized Maximin and held him over the abyss and screamed at him: "I will drop you here and now if you don't admit that all you have told us is false." The petrified Maximin refused to recant.

"There are many anecdotes showing these young illiterates facing antagonists and puncturing objections with a witty, lightning-quick answer. All were amazed. They alone were emotionless, as if strangers to their own words.

> "A parish priest (in the nearby diocese of Gap) said to Melanie: "The Lady disappeared in a cloud!"
>
> Melanie: "There was no cloud."
>
> The parish priest insists: "But it is easy to wrap oneself in a cloud and disappear!"
>
> Melanie: "Sir, wrap yourself up in a cloud and disappear!"
>
> Another priest said to Maximin: "Aren't you tired, little one, of having to repeat the same thing every day?" Maximin: "And you, Sir, do you get tired of saying Mass every day?"

Father Jean Jaouen, a Missionary of La Salette, wrote in a book recently published in English:

> "What will these poor, innocent children of La Salette meet on the road this first step is taking them? Tomorrow they will feel the Pastor's heartfelt enthusiasm, but tomorrow also they will be in the public eye and the targets of dull-witted jokes

(the Corps dignitaries addressing Maximin: "Oh! The Blessed Virgin's son!"). Still tomorrow, they would face endless interrogations with the usual traps, threats and tricks. "Here, take these twenty francs for your relatives; they won't have to beg any more," suggested Mayor Peytard to Melanie. "You can have them if you promise to keep quiet." Soon, in the matter of a few weeks, they would find it impossible to be themselves, to live the lives of children like other boys and girls their age. The hordes of the curious invading Corps would harass them at the Sisters' house where the bishop intended to give them a peaceful hideaway. As adults, they wandered from one place to the next, without resources or steady income, tossed about by the world's harshness as well as by their own weaknesses.

"Beneath the unstable lives and their fragile inner equilibrium the underlying evil that had befallen them was easily recognizable: they had been uprooted. "The apparition has not changed us, it has left us with all our faults," Maximin acknowledged. No doubt. Still, their defects would not have brought on the same consequences and the children would have more easily found their own balance had they remained in their native mountains, yielding only to the laws of the earth and to the ways of a simple life. Uprooted, they would become defenseless against their own erratic moods, an overwrought imagination and seductions of all kinds that lay in wait for witnesses of a celestial vision. The temporal failure of their lives is one result. Those who sought their welfare and those who exploited them have contributed to it as much as their own shortcomings.

"But, at the source of it all, there was the apparition.

Without the obligation it placed upon them to bear witness to it they would have remained what they were, carefree children, inheritors of a peaceful destiny.

"Should we pity them and ask her to explain why she chose them for such a challenging honor? Let us rather think of the mystery of La Salette. The Virgin who can no longer restrain the arm of her Son had need of the suffering of her young witnesses as a humble complement to her own suffering and self-offering.

"One thing is certain. They were the instruments of a grace which, after more than a hundred years is still alive. Through them, by the simple account they gave to their masters in the evening of September 19, 1846, the Apparition of La Salette passed into history. Henceforth, it will be felt in the lives of people. It will stamp the piety of the Church with apostolic and mystical orientations. It will shape the obscure destinies of humanity. The anxiety of a Baptiste Pra, the muted awakening of conscience and of faith in the first hearers of the Great News were but a hint of the wonders yet to come. It was the quiet, invisible source of grace that one day would flood the world." (18)

Why is this message so important? Why were Maximin and Melanie told to make it known to the entire world? First, the message concerns Christ himself. By her apparition the Lady clearly glorifies her Son and reminds the whole world of his abiding presence in the world. The Lady's message is highly biblical in tone. It concerns Christ, his holy Name. It concerns the Eucharist, unceasing prayer and the Lord's Day. It reminds all of the duty of penance for the pursuit of Christian life.

These tenets may very well appear elementary and basic. The theology here is light years from sophistication. And yet, we know that a Christian who lives wholly by these injunctions can attain the highest degree of holiness.

If the Lady is again bringing Christ to the world, it follows that she is also bringing love to all her people. And one can label love basic, primary and elementary. When the love of Christ is involved, it always suffices. It is enough.

A Few Concluding Words

The tears of the Lady at La Salette proclaim that we are not God's hobby—we are God's passion.

THE MYSTERIOUS TEARS OF THE MOTHER OF GOD AT LA SALETTE are a testimony to God's concern for humankind's wellbeing. La Salette is one more instance of God's anger at seeing God's people deliberately causing their own misery and pain. (The children understood the symbol of tears immediately).

Human tears are both a sign and a reality. There is no doubt that these tears were meant to impress. Tears are always the visible signs of trauma or of the profound experience of joy. In any case they indicate an extreme emotion. They are the most visible signs, the most telltale and the most authentic of what is happening within a person. The tears of Our Lady at La Salette are commonly understood as expressing profound sadness. They are a sign that the weeping person has reached the limit of his or her capacity to conceal pain. The flood of distress has reached the point of overflow and affliction becomes "flesh" spilling down the face in streams of liquid heartache.

At La Salette the tears of Our Lady are a sign. The tears flowing down Mary's face are also part of the message she brought to the world in 1846. The children said that she wept all the time she was giving her discourse. The tears are part of that discourse and they become the unspoken message of La Salette. They are in a real sense the tears of God because the whole message of La Salette is from God. They express God's dissatisfaction, God's anger and sadness, especially God's concern for people. Ours is a caring God and tears are a sublime code-sign for personal and profound distress over God's people. The tears that fell here are falling on the earth forever.

It does no harm to the reconciler to have the gift of tears since he or she must show concern for people. I remember preaching a parish mission in upstate New York, a region where many Roman Catholics had been going over to Protestant denominations, especially the Church of God. The church walls were barely keeping out the skin-cracking Arctic cold as the pastor said: "People are leaving the Church because it is too cold, and I am not referring to the weather outside. People are going over to the Protestant churches because the climate there is warmer. People come to Mass on Sunday here because they have to. People go to those churches across the way because they like to go there. We Catholics must get to like to come to church because we feel wanted here, because we feel that God cares for us here, because pastor and people actually care about us and like to see us. Our Catholic Church has to warm up."

Tears are Warmth

Any apparition of Our Lady has one purpose: to relate Christ to his people. There can be no other incentive. Mary always acts and speaks in relation to him. This is her role in all of the New Testament. Without him she would not be who she is. The sole reason for La Salette is to recall the presence of Christ among his people. In a special way it is to bring out his concern and his anxiety for this people. The first words Our Lady uttered were: "Come near, my children, be not afraid. I am here to bring you great news." She spoke for someone, in someone's name. In this case, the news is not transmitted solely by the use of words but also by an attitude, a state of mind and heart, an outward show of displeasure and sorrow that reflect the Lord's own mind. The sorrow she manifests at La Salette is the Lord's sorrow. The tears reflect the Lord's attitude toward his people.

No one can say that La Salette is a cold, colorless apparition. Our Lady did not appear on this high mountain to hand down a few warnings and prescribe prayers and practices. There is nothing calm and cold about this event.

The children, Maximin and Melanie, saw her sitting on a stone, her face in her hands, and she was weeping. Tears are always an overflow. They are pressured out of the heart by an excess of pain or joy. This is a case of pure pain.

Tears are not a merely physiological reality. They are also, as is the case here, signs of loving concern. Christ wept over Jerusalem because He was concerned. People weep because they care. Tears are the opposite of fish-coldness, indifference, disinterest and apathy. They signal involvement and the intense will to be part of another person's life.

These tears are La Salette's most powerful unspoken message. The beautiful Lady weeps but she never refers to her tears, never so much as alludes to them. They are meant to speak for themselves, and they do. They are an unspoken message but they add a crucial dimension to her words. When we read the message of La Salette we remember that it was spoken by someone in tears. Without the tears, the "a capella" words would take on an icy aloofness, even a kind of muffled ferocity. The words she spoke had to be spoken. The Lady's 'problem' was how to communicate this sad news without sowing worldwide panic and the threat of Armageddon by famine instead of fire.

Teachers always say that one can do whatever one pleases with children as long as they know you love them. You can tell them anything as long as they see proven love behind the hard words. The Lady's sign of affection, the universally accepted sign of a mother's desperate love, has always been tears. At La Salette, they are liquid sorrow, molten streams of pain running down the Lady's face and a very obvious show of love.

Whoever reads the message or speaks about it must remember to place the tough message in the context of the care and affection made evident by the Lady's abiding sorrow.

The tears should be remembered for another reason. They highlight the words and give urgency and crucial importance to the entire message. If someone from heaven, and the Blessed Virgin at that, is provoked to tears over disrespect for the Day of the Lord and the Name of Jesus, then the word is out that these offenses are more evil than people think they are and should be carefully avoided.

And then, there is the following point: if the words she speaks are a message from her Son, then why wouldn't the tears themselves communicate something from the very Person of Christ. If her words are a reflection of his will then why shouldn't the tears mirror God's own care and affection? The Woman speaks the words of Christ. Why wouldn't she weep the tears of God?

La Salette and Laity

THERE IS SOMETHING SPECIAL ABOUT THE MESSAGE of La Salette that dawns on the reader like a surprise. The hierarchy—the priesthood, the clergy in any form or capacity—are never mentioned. Maximin and Melanie were lay people. The Lady spoke of "my people" by which we presume she meant the entire world. She mentioned elderly women who were the only ones at Mass on Sundays; she spoke of Maximin's papa as well as of the farmer of Coin. She spoke of cart drivers and of "children under seven years of age" who "will be seized with trembling and die in the arms of those holding them."

The emergence of the layperson has been and continues to be one of the most important and the most visible characteristics of the postconciliar Church. The phrase "the emerging layman" has been with us since the early sixties-even the sexist language (layman) smacks of that period. The notion is intimately connected with that of church: the Church is essentially composed of laypeople. Laity now share in the Liturgy of the Word from the sanctuary. They distribute the bread of the Eucharist, they serve on parish councils and on archdiocesan and diocesan committees and they teach in our seminaries. This is not token improvement. This is not paper-clip change. This is ongoing reconciliation.

We remember when the priest called his people "the populo (the people)." This may sound strange today but at the time it was said, such a remark was symptomatic: it took for granted a clear separation between Church and laity, or between clergy and laity. The communion rail was more than a symbolic table. It was a fence.

The assimilation of the laity into the life of the Church will take years to run its course. This is probably just as well. The slow pace will solidify change, deepen it, and ward off tokenism. But reconciliation is very present, and we are all aware of the process nature of reconciliation. Wherever we have spoken of the laity previously, we have understood both men and women. Women, religious sisters are speaking from the pulpit, teaching in seminaries, preaching and directing retreats and spiritual exercises. All of this was inconceivable twenty-five years ago.

We see here how the concept of reconciliation does not deal only with whatever is sinful and alienates people from God. It also deals with situations and conditions of social and cultural alienation and helps change them in order to bring people together to work and pray together. Reconciliation changes the Church, both local and universal into a gathering of gifts.

Another factor accounting for the emergence of lay people is the dearth of vocations to the priesthood. Lay people will of necessity be brought into the active, ministerial, liturgical and administrative life of the Church in ever-greater numbers. These people will bring their professional competence as well as their spiritual gifts and the reconciliation will deepen and continue to enrich and sanctify the Church.

The strongest and most profound basis for the emergence of the layperson lies less in social factors than in the Gospel call to follow Christ. The pursuit of spiritual perfection is no longer (it never was) the exclusive domain of religious or priest but the privilege and duty of everyone.

Clearly, Christ was addressing the crowds in the Sermon on the Mount of the gospel of Matthew.

'When he saw the crowds, he went up the mountain, and after he had sat down, his disciples came to him. He began to teach them, saying..." (Mt. 5:1-2) In the same Sermon Christ, addressing the same people, said: "You have heard that it was said, 'You shall love your neighbor and hate your enemy.' But I say to you, love your enemies, and pray for those who persecute you, that you may be children of your heavenly Father....For if you love those who love you, what recompense will you have?...So be perfect, just as your heavenly Father is perfect." (Matthew 5: 43-46, 48)

The presence of the crowds makes it plain that the ideal of Christian perfection as described and commanded in the Gospel of Matthew belongs to everyone.

Our Lady of La Salette appeared to two peasant children-working children, "lay children", children of the people. Her discourse was a message to her people. "You will make this known to all my people", she said and repeated to Maximin and Melanie. Nowhere in he discourse is there any allusion to clergy or hierarchy. During her assumption she turned in the direction of Rome, but this was a symbolic gesture and she did not include it in her discourse.

This same discourse was a clear appeal to the perfection of the Christian life addressed to lay people. There was a call to the Eucharist. A call to prayer. A call to penance. A call to conversion. A call to suffering. A call to honor the name of Jesus and to the observance of Sunday as a day to be offered to God. (19)

The concerns she addressed in her discourse were laypeople's concerns: the harvest; decaying wheat, rotting walnuts and raisins. She jogged Maximin's memory relative to a long forgotten conversation with his father at the farm of Coin. This father and son conversation was a layperson's dialogue. Maximin reminded his discontented father that the Lady had spoken of him in her discourse. The next day, Monsieur Giraud was healed of a sickness and returned to the practice of religion.

The Lady excludes no one from the concern of her tears and her suffering. She is speaking to all her people. But an overview of the La Salette event quickly establishes it as strongly directed toward the laity.

ENDNOTES

1. LeBoeuf, Michael, Ph.D., *How to Win Customers and Keep Them for Life*. Berkeley, by arrangement with G. P. Putnam's Sons, March 1989, pp. 34-35.

2. Jaouen, Jean, M.S., *A Grace Called La Salette*. Grassroots Publishing International, Enfield, NH, 1991, pg. 41.

3. Luther, Martin, 1483-1546, *The table talk of Martin Luther*. Edited with an introduction by Thomas S. Kepler, Dover Edition, 2005.

4. Leseur Elizabeth, *Journal et pensées de chaque jour*, Paris, 1918, p. 31.

5. John Paul II, Pope, *Apostolic Exhortation on Reconciliation and Penance*, Dec. 2, 1984, #16.

6. Barclay, William, *Daily Celebration*, 2. Word Books, Publisher, 1973, pp. 81-82.

7. Heschel, Abraham Joshua, *Man's Quest for God*, Aurora Printers, 1998, p. 35-36

8. Buttrick, George Arthur, *The Interpreter's Bible, Vol. 2: Leviticus, Numbers, Deuteronomy, Joshua, Judges, Ruth*. Abington Press, June, 1953, pg. 50.

9. Job, Rueben P., and Norman Shawchuck, *A Guide to Prayer for Ministers and Other Servants*. The Upper Room, Nashville, Tennessee, pp. 63-64, which quotes *From Spirituality for Ministry*, by Urban T. Holmes III.

10. Forest, Jim, *Making Friends of Enemies: Reflections of the Teachings of Jesus*. Crossroad, N.Y., 1989, p. 27.

11. Nouwen, Henri J. M., *The Living Reminder: Service and Prayers in Memory of Jesus Christ*, HarperOne, 2009.

12. Heschel, *The Quest for God*, pp. 36-37.

13. Bausch, Fr. William J., *Take Heart, Father: A Hope-Filled Vision for Today's Priest*. Twenty-Third Publications, p. 31.

14. Bausch, *Take Heart, Father: A Hope-Filled Vision for Today's Priest*.

15. Jaouen, *A Grace Called La Salette*, p. 294.

16. Jones, Allan, *Passion for Pilgrimage*. Harper & Row, 1989, p. 90.

17. Barclay, William, *Daily Celebration, 2.* Word Books, Publisher, 1973, p. 97.

18. Jaouen, Jean, M.S., *A Grace Called La Salette*. Grassroots Publishing International, Enfield, NH, 1991, pp. 5-7.

19. Giraud, P. Silvain-Marie, M.S., *Le livre des exercices spirituels de Notre-Dame de La Salette*, 1861, pp. 294-345.